CONSTRUCTIVE THINKING

How to **Grow** Beyond Your **Mind**

LISA MANZI LENTINO, PH.D.

Grow Beyond Your Mind, LLC

Constructive Thinking
How to Grow Beyond Your Mind
Lisa Manzi Lentino, Ph.D.

Published by Grow Beyond Your Mind Press, Sudbury, MA

Limit of Liability/Disclaimer of Warranty: While the publisher and author have used their best efforts in preparing this book, they make no representations or warranties with respect to the accuracy or completeness of the contents of this book and specifically disclaim any implied warranties of merchantability or fitness for a particular purpose. No warranty may be created or extended by sales representatives or written sales materials. Neither the publisher nor author shall be liable for any loss of profit or any other commercial damages, including but not limited to special, incidental, consequential, or other damages.

The material contained in this book is intended to provide helpful and informative material on the subject addressed. It is sold with the understanding that the author and publisher are not engaged in rendering psychological, financial, legal or other professional services. Any use of the information contained in this book is at the reader's discretion. This book is not intended to serve as a replacement for professional medical or psychological advice. If expert assistance or counseling is needed, the services of a competent professional should be sought.

Index: Elena Gwynne, www.quillandinkindexing.com
Cover and Interior design: Davis Creative, www.daviscreative.com
Cover copy: Tracy Carlson, www.rightbrainbrands .com

Library of Congress Control Number: 2014911257
ISBN: 978-0-9905266-0-5

ATTENTION CORPORATIONS, UNIVERSITIES, COLLEGES AND PROFESSIONAL ORGANIZATIONS: Quantity discounts are available on bulk purchases of this book for educational, gift purposes, or as premiums for increasing magazine subscriptions or renewals. Special books or book excerpts can also be created to fit specific needs. For information, please contact info@growbeyondyourmind.com

DEDICATION

This book is dedicated to anyone who has ever had an inkling that "there's got to be a better way," or a gnawing feeling that there's something else you're supposed to be doing with your life. It's for anyone who would like to feel more engaged in life and have a deeper connection with themselves and others. It's also for those who would like to discover, develop and share their natural talents with the world.

Contents

List of Illustrations

Acknowledgments

I would first like to thank all of those from whose work I have benefitted and been enlightened. Some have directly contributed to this book, while others have been instrumental in my development and ideas more generally. These individuals include: James Allen, Herbert Benson, Edmund Bourne, David Burns, Dale Carnegie, Steven Covey, Carol Dweck, Tim Gallwey, Rick Hanson, Russ Harris, Steven Hayes, Jon Kabat-Zinn, Marsha Linehan, Bruce Lipton, Orison Marden, Thomas Marra, John Maxwell, Daniel Pink, Jim Rohn, Marshall Rosenberg, Hans Selye, Daniel Siegel, Eckhart Tolle and Wallace Wattles. I am grateful for being able to grow and learn from these authors and many others on a daily basis.

I would also like to thank Vonda at First Editing, Alyssa Graybeal and Jason Manganaro for their assistance with editing. Michael Lovett and Alex Klein of Lovett Design completed the illustrations. I am grateful for both their patience and ability to capture the concepts I presented visually. I am also grateful to Mrs. Kelly for her encouragement and taking the time to review my manuscript. The book design was completed by Davis Creative and production was coordinated by Janica Smith, I am sincerely thankful for their care and expertise.

I would also like to express my appreciation for my husband Joe and his continuous support of all my ideas and endeavors, and my children, Elizabeth and Nicholas, for their patience, support and listening to Mom talk about "the mind" all the time. I am also always grateful for my parents and their support throughout the years.

Introduction

What is constructive thinking?

Constructive thinking is the ability to consistently engage thoughts that help you manifest the life you were meant to live while at the same time disregarding those that hinder, or worse, sabotage, your growth and progress. The thoughts that you engage on a daily basis (the habits in the way you think) are one of the most powerful factors contributing to how your life will turn out. However, most of us were never taught to become conscious of the way we think or to harness the power of our thinking. Instead, the majority of us go through life blindly listening to the thought patterns we inherited while growing up, which are often not conducive to or ideal for our growth and development. The process of becoming a true constructive thinker involves learning to become much more conscious of the programming you acquired from childhood and how your thoughts may be trapping you and keeping you from fulfilling your potential. Freeing yourself from your dysfunctional programming is one of the most crucial steps toward manifesting your ideal life. Once free, you are able to observe yourself more genuinely and discover your true purpose. From the vantage point of your true self, you are then positioned to generate and engage only constructive thought patterns that help you manifest the life you were meant to live. It is my sincere hope that this book will empower you with the awareness, knowledge and tools to embark on a journey toward becoming a true constructive thinker and to grow your life in a way you may have never conceived. Let's begin your journey by looking at the first step toward becoming a constructive thinker.

Phase One

·················

Freeing the
Real You from
Your Mind's Programming

Thoroughly Understanding That You Are Not Your Mind

Some of you reading this statement may already understand this concept. If so, I give you credit for already getting to this level of insight, and I'm sure your life has already benefitted significantly from this level of understanding. For those of you who are somewhat (or thoroughly) confused by what I mean by the statement "You are not your mind," let me try to explain.

If you think about the day you were born, what was really there on that day? There was a unique consciousness or awareness (a YOU, if you will) that came into the world and started checking out these "big people" and your surroundings. That unique consciousness comes into the world with two incredible tools at its disposal: your body and the database of your mind (Tolle, 1999).

I will be going into much greater detail about the database of your mind, but for now I want to focus on the unique consciousness. First, what exactly is this unique consciousness? For one, it is the true essence of who you really are—which unfortunately, many of us lose sight of over the course of our lives. Some may refer to it as our soul or the place from which we can connect to a larger power, be it God, a universal energy or a more general larger consciousness. It is the place from which our intuition or "gut" feelings arise. It is the place from which, if we actually learn to listen, our true purpose in this world is revealed (Tolle, 1999).

I like to use the metaphor of an acorn to more fully explain the concept of our unique consciousness. An acorn comes into this world with the full potential of an oak tree contained within its shell. To what extent that acorn manifests its full potential depends upon the soil it lands in, how much water and sun it has access to, and how many other trees are overpowering it. The same is true for a newborn. The day we enter the world, each of us comes with a unique set of potentials that only we can bring to the world. Contained within our infant bodies are all of our physical, intellectual, athletic, artistic and musical potentials just waiting to be nurtured. To what extent we manifest those potentials depends largely upon the environments in which we grow up or those we later create for ourselves as adults—as well as the extent to which we get trapped by our minds.

It's also important to note that no matter what, an acorn is never going to grow up to be a maple or pine or any tree other than what it was intended to be: an oak tree. Similarly, too many of us not only lose sight of what's in our acorn; we then go on a wild-goose chase trying to live our lives being like other people—an endeavor that is truly as fruitless as a young oak tree spending all its time and energy trying to be like a nearby pine or maple. This tendency is just one example of the many ways the database of our mind ends up trapping us. Therefore, our next step is to start examining this database more closely so we can begin to understand the many ways in which it all too often limits us from fully developing and finding true contentment in this world.

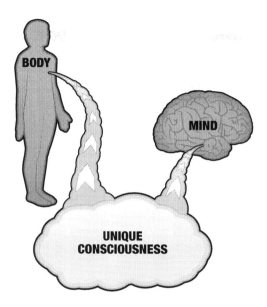

FIGURE 1: The relationship between the unique consciousness, the body
and the ego/database

Separating The Real You
From The Database

After reading step one, I hope you have a better understanding of what I mean when I refer to the real YOU versus the database of your mind. Below is a chart to help you more fully understand the definitions of these concepts. Remember, when we are referring to a "unique consciousness," we are referring to the consciousness (or awareness) that was there the day you were born (Tolle, 1999). It is the YOU that was looking out from behind your infant eyes starting the day you came into this world. It is the same YOU that continues to observe life from behind your eyes as an adult. Because that consciousness is the true essence of who you are, it does not fundamentally change throughout your lifetime. What does change dramatically throughout your lifetime is the database of your mind. The database starts collecting information about the world from the moment you're born (and well before that, most agree) and changes exponentially throughout your life. That database is a collection of our thoughts, beliefs, memories, emotional reactions, knowledge and neural pathways that we have accumulated. Its original purpose was to help us survive and navigate the world successfully so that we could ultimately fulfill our purpose in the world. Unfortunately, instead of helping our cause, all too often our own minds end up becoming our greatest obstacles to living the life we were meant to live. I will explain how this process happens shortly, but first read the chart below to gain a better understanding of what I mean by "unique consciousness" versus the "database of our mind."

Unique consciousness:
- The YOU (awareness) that began observing the world the day were born
- Contains the true essence of who you are and your ultimate purpose in life
- Like an acorn, contains all the potential of who you could possibly be
- Place from which our intuition and "gut" feelings arise
- Place from which we connect on a more spiritual level

Database of our mind:
- A collection of thoughts, beliefs, memories, emotional reactions and neural pathways collected from our experiences, beginning at birth (as well as later stages of pregnancy)
- Designed to help ensure our safety and survival (not yet well-designed for our happiness)
- Was supposed to be a tool for us to manifest who we really are but all too often ends up trapping us

Understanding How The Database Collects And Stores Information

What is the database really good at?

The database of our mind is one of the most incredible survival and problem-solving machines ever created. It has proven remarkably successful in helping we humans ensure our safety, survive and procreate our species. It is extremely efficient at collecting, storing and retrieving information, as well as recognizing patterns and learning from past experiences—particularly when it even remotely perceives a potential threat to our well-being.

What is the database not-so-good at?

A common misconception people have about our mind is that because it is so good at helping us survive, it should be equally good at helping us find happiness in life. Unfortunately, this is simply not the case. If left to its own devices, our mind will choose our safety and survival over our happiness any day. It is simply not yet well designed for our happiness. The reason for this is that our minds have not caught up to the evolutionary fact that we're no longer in the wilderness and no longer need to be wary of wild animals or hunt for our food. A reality with grocery stores and homes with luxuries like electricity and indoor plumbing has been such a small and recent blip in human history that our mind has not yet been able to fully incorporate it into the way it's designed. It's so important to understand our mind's priorities, because if it deems that something could potentially be dangerous—like relationships, for example—it will do all it possibly can (often unconsciously) to get you to avoid or sabotage them. If your unconscious mind believes relationships are potentially threatening, it would much rather you be lonely and safe for the rest of your life. I will be talking much more about this process and how to override it later on.

How do our minds get all this information into the database?

As Dan Siegel (2012) explains, there are two memory systems that our minds use to get information into the database. The first is what most people are referring to when they say they're remembering something. That memory system is called our "explicit memory." Our explicit memory is our conscious memory. Therefore, when we are remembering something from our explicit memory, we are aware of the fact that we are remembering it and that there is distance between that event and the present moment. In order for us to do that, at some point in time we had to pay conscious attention to what it was we were remembering. So for instance, if I'm remembering what my grade school building looked like, I'm consciously calling up that memory, I'm aware that I'm doing it, and I know there's quite a bit of distance between grade school and now. In order for me to do this, at some point in time I needed to consciously pay attention to what my grade school building looked like. I can thank my explicit memory for this. In terms of timing, this memory system doesn't fully come on board until around age 2-4, when language skills begin to develop, which is why we don't have conscious memories from our first year of life.

The other memory system that we have, which tends to make our lives more interesting, is called our "implicit memory." Our implicit memory is our unconscious memory, but when I say unconscious, don't think of Freud's repressed unconscious memories. Instead, think of it like a "subconscious" memory system. For example, if you drove a car today, unless you are a novice driver, you didn't have to think about every step in driving your car or how to get to a routine location. You can thank your implicit memory for being able to do such things.

What are the differences between our explicit and implicit memory systems?

There are several key differences between our explicit and implicit memories that we need to be aware of in order to understand how to operate our mind most effectively. First, while our explicit memory doesn't come on board until around age 2-4, our implicit memory is there from the time we are born, and most people say well before that. From our earliest moments, our implicit memory is constantly collecting information like a sponge, continually soaking in everything it can from our environment (what we see, hear, feel, experience internally, etc.). Therefore, while we need to pay conscious attention to get information into our explicit memory, our implicit memory collects information without the need for focused attention. Another important difference is that when we remember something from our explicit memory, we are aware that we are actually calling up a memory. However, when an implicit memory is triggered we are often not even aware that we are remembering something (our unconscious mind is doing that all on its own). This is how our implicit memory ends up influencing our lives all the time without us even realizing it!

Our explicit and implicit memories also differ in several important ways having to do with size, speed and the way information is organized. While most of us would probably like to think that our explicit, conscious mind controls the majority of the database of our mind, the exact opposite is true. Our conscious, explicit memory is a mere 10-15% of the database. Therefore, our implicit memory, operating largely without us consciously knowing what it's doing, dominates about 90% of our minds! Why would evolution design it so our conscious mind is so small relative to our unconscious mind? One reason is that our conscious explicit memory system is much more rational and logical than our implicit unconscious memory, but the trade-off to being more rational is that our explicit memory is relatively slow and can only take in a limited amount of information. The reality is that our conscious memory can only perceive a sliver of the actual amount of information in our environment. If our species had to rely solely on our conscious, explicit memory, we probably would not have fared very well, especially in the wilderness. Luckily for us, our implicit memory is an incredibly fast, efficient data-collecting machine with the capacity to collect huge amounts of information. For this reason, it has played a crucial role in our survival as a species.

However, the major drawback to our implicit memory is that it often falls short with regard to being rational or logical. While our explicit memory tends to think about things more logically and organize information based on linear timelines (such as re-calling events of our life story), our implicit memory collects and organizes information based on associations (which may or may not be logical) and common themes. If you've taken any Psychology class you may recall Pavlov's experiments with dogs in which he paired a bell with food. The dogs learned to salivate to the sound of the bell because it had been associated with food that naturally caused salivation. That's how our implicit memory works. Now in certain situations that strategy may work very well. For example, the sound of a growl may be associated with an angry animal and the need for escape that is quite logical. However, consider the example of a certain song playing on the radio when someone's girlfriend or boyfriend broke up with them. As far as our implicit mind is concerned, that particular song on the radio becomes "dangerous" because of its associations with the painful emotions of the breakup. Hopefully you are beginning to see how our implicit mind (although well-intentioned) could easily send us astray.

Explicit Memory

- Develops around age 2 (when language starts developing)
- What people are generally referring to when they say they're remembering something
- Requires conscious attention - you need to consciously focus your attention on something in order to get it into your explicit memory
- Involves a part of our brain called the hippocampus which helps package our memories and gives them a sense of having a beginning and an end
- When an explicit memory is triggered, we are aware we are calling up something from the past and we have a sense of distance between when that event happened and the present moment
- Involves episodic memories - memories of the experiences which make up our life story and factual memories - information which contributes to our overall knowledge base about ourselves, others and the world around us

Implicit Memory

- Present from the moment we are born (and most agree even before that)
- Does not require conscious attention
- Does not require the hippocampus
- When an implicit memory is triggered, we don't have the sense that we are "remembering" something - we are generally not even aware that material from our implicit memory is being recalled by our mind
- Plays a very important role in keeping us safe and ensuring our survival
- Continually collects information for us and does its job of forming associations, creating mental models and helping us anticipate the future
- Can make our lives more interesting/challenging without us even realizing it

FIGURE 2: Characteristics of explicit and implicit memory

How does our implicit memory organize the information it collects?

As our implicit mind collects all this information and starts forming associations, it then organizes the data based on larger themes such as relationships, conflict, emotions, stress, work, etc. Think about the implicit mind as a huge 3-D spider web network of neural associations. The different themes are organized according to different "sections" of the database, if you will. What's really important to understand is that the implicit mind does not organize information based on linear time or chronology, but instead, on associations and common themes. This is why many people are confused as to why something that may have happened 20-30 plus years ago still bothers them. As far as the implicit mind is concerned, time is irrelevant. A threat is a threat—it doesn't matter if it happened decades ago or a few seconds ago. From a survival standpoint, this strategy has served us well; from a happiness standpoint, not so much.

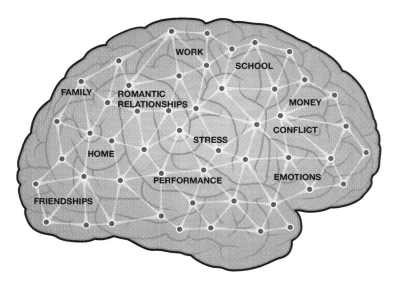

FIGURE 3: 3D model of neural associations and diagram of "departments"

Because the implicit memory is not organized along a linear timeline, one of the things it is not good at is contextually updating an association. Let me explain. Say for example, a young infant is bitten by a dog. Although he has no conscious memory of the experience, his implicit memory most certainly does and records that "dogs are dangerous." Because of its priority for safety and its need for speed when gathering and assessing information, it's also important to note that our implicit mind has the tendency to make blanket statements and over-generalize (again, this makes sense from a safety/survival standpoint but not from the standpoint of our happiness). So instead of concluding that a specific dog on a specific day was dangerous, the implicit memory over-generalizes that "all dogs are dangerous." With this belief in the implicit database, it's not a surprise that this young boy would develop a dog phobia as he gets older. Let's say, then, this boy grows into a man, gets married and has a family of his own, and his kids approach him wanting a dog. His implicit memory still has the idea that "dogs are dangerous" but has not taken into consideration that he's an adult man over six-feet tall and would only consider getting a family-friendly dog. This is what I mean when I say the implicit mind does not contextually update an association. As far as it's concerned, the grown man is still as vulnerable to a dog as he was when he was an infant.

Again, I hope you are starting to see that while our implicit memory has many advantages from an evolutionary perspective, it has many shortcomings as well: it bases its conclusions on associations (rather than logical reasoning), it tends to over-generalize and it doesn't take time into consideration and contextually update associations. These shortcomings are going to be important to remember as we take a closer look at what the implicit mind does with all the information it collects and how it traps us, which is where our next step begins.

Understanding How The Database Forms Mental Models

How does our mind develop mental models?

In order to truly free yourself from your mind, you first have to understand what our implicit mind does with the information it collects, because this is the first step in how it ends up trapping us. As Dan Siegel explains, as a baby begins to grow its implicit mind is collecting and organizing information according to themes and associations, and it starts to form mental models based on interpretations it makes as to how the world works.

Let's look at an example of how a mental model may be formed. Picture a baby girl on the day she is born. She starts experiencing the bodily sensation of hunger, is distressed and naturally begins to cry. If the baby is fortunate, she will have a responsive parent who comforts her and meets her needs by feeding her—if so, all is right with the world. While the baby will have no conscious recollection of this day when she gets older, her implicit memory will certainly have recorded her introduction into this huge world and these "big people." If she remotely perceived any threat or danger, her implicit memory would be sure to record and hold onto this information. Again, because our mind's top priority is our safety and survival, not our happiness, it will have a stronger tendency to notice and store potentially threatening or emotionally charged memories rather than pleasant or neutral ones. In our example, the baby's mind will start forming mental models of Mom or Dad as comforting, trustworthy and dependable if her needs are usually met when she's distressed, and the opposite if her needs are not met.

So the first step is that our implicit memory collects information and forms associations, then uses these associations to form mental models. In our example, it may look something like the following:

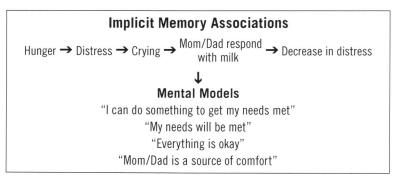

Implicit Memory Associations

Hunger → Distress → Crying → Mom/Dad respond with milk → Decrease in distress

↓

Mental Models

"I can do something to get my needs met"
"My needs will be met"
"Everything is okay"
"Mom/Dad is a source of comfort"

Especially in our early years, our mind is forming countless numbers of these models in order to try and navigate our world as best as it possibly can. Think about it for a second: beyond some basic instincts, human infants are thrust into this world with little information on how it actually operates. From the time we are born, the mind is on a mission to collect as much information as possible so it can construct road maps, if you will, of how to best navigate our way in the world. Mental models are one of our mind's first strategies for doing just that. Let's take a little closer look at how our mind actually uses these mental models.

What does our mind do with these mental models?

Now that you have some understanding of how these mental models are formed, the next important thing to understand is how they change our perception of everything in our environment, including ourselves. Think about these mental models as lenses through which we observe everything, from ourselves to others and the world—just like eyeglass lenses. Now the thing to remember about a lens is that it ends up filtering everything you view through it. How exactly it filters everything depends upon how it is designed (just as there are different prescription strengths for eyeglass lenses). So while we might think that when we are observing something or someone we are seeing them as they actually are, in truth, our mental models (formed largely from our childhood and early experiences) constantly alter our perceptions of everything, and we don't even realize it!

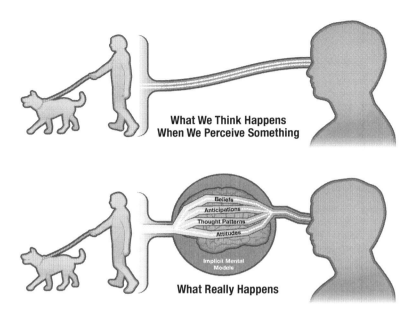

Figure 4: How our beliefs act as mental filters

Once a mental model is in place, our mind tries to use it to help its mission of keeping us safe and navigating the world effectively. It uses these mental models to anticipate or predict what is going to happen in a particular situation and then to prime us to behave or respond in a particular way. Take a minute to think about how important it is for you to be able to predict someone else's behavior or what's going to happen in a situation if you are the one in charge of someone's safety. For example, let's say you had two dogs and it was your job to keep you and someone else safe from them. One dog was very snappy and would often growl whenever you approached. The other appeared very mild-mannered and friendly but one day, out of the blue, he snapped at you. Which dog are you actually more comfortable around if you're in charge of safety? Ironically, most people would choose the predictably aggressive one because at least we know what to expect and we could then behave accordingly. Most of us would be more upset by being snapped at by the mild-mannered dog because that behavior wouldn't have been consistent with what we would have predicted—we would have been caught off guard, which is something our mind really doesn't like.

Let's take a moment to review the steps involved with mental models. First, our mind collects information and organizes it based on associations. It then forms mental models based on these interpretations. The last step, then, is that it uses these mental models as lenses through which we see the world and subsequently primes us to anticipate experiences and behave in certain ways. So to go back to our example of the baby girl, her experiences of what her parents do when she's hungry lead her to form certain mental models, which then prime her to behave in certain ways when she's hungry. Take a look below to see how this process might work.

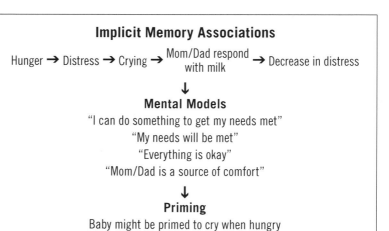

Hopefully you are starting to develop some understanding of the dynamics of how our experiences influence the mental models we form, which in turn influence our perception of ourselves and the environment, and subsequently how we behave or approach the world. This dynamic becomes even more powerful as we start developing language around the age of 2-3. Let's now take a look at how language becomes such a powerful force in determining what kind of lives we live.

Understanding How Our Core Beliefs Are Formed

From the time we are born, our mind is an incredible data-collecting machine and has the ability to help us navigate the world by forming mental models. But as we develop the ability to form words and use language, our mind becomes much more powerful because it can use words to form our thoughts about the world.

With language, young children start putting words to the mental models and interpretations their young minds create. As their thoughts start to accumulate, they develop what we refer to as "core beliefs" about themselves, relationships and the world in general (Burns, 1999). These core beliefs play such a crucial role in our lives because (just like our earlier mental models) they serve as the lenses through which we perceive everything in our lives, including ourselves. Think about our core beliefs as the initial "programming" of our mind, if you will. They involve fundamental topics such as our worth and value as a person, how safe we are in the world, whether relationships are a source of pain or comfort, and what emotions are all about. The nature of our core beliefs reflects the quality of all the interactions we have with our physical and social environment, beginning from the earliest stages of our life. Therefore, our programming reflects the relative health or dysfunction of our parents, siblings, friends, teachers, coaches, other relatives, as well as our society and larger culture (including the TV shows, media and other influences to which we are exposed). So based on how our early years progressed, we could have developed core beliefs similar to the following:

The world
"The world is a generally safe place to live." OR "The world is a place to be wary of."

Our worth
"I'm lovable."   OR "I'm only lovable if I behave a certain way."

Relationships
"People are comforting."   OR "People can be scary and unpredictable."

Emotions
"Emotions are a normal part of life."   OR "Emotions are scary and need to be
                                              avoided."

Conflict
"Conflict is natural in relationships."   OR "Conflict is hurtful and destructive."

The reason these beliefs are so important is not only that they serve as lenses through which we perceive ourselves and the world, but subsequently they also give rise to our habitual thought patterns during our daily lives. Our thoughts become that internal dialogue or voice in our heads that we carry with us throughout the day. As our discussion continues, the crucial role our thoughts and beliefs play in creating our lives will become much clearer, but for now just be aware of the connection between our experiences, core beliefs and patterns of thinking, as the chart below describes:

So as we develop, the database of our mind first starts filling with mental models of ourselves and the world. Then as language develops, our mind starts forming thoughts, core beliefs, patterns in the way we think, and that voice in our heads. With language, the database becomes a much more powerful tool for helping our unique consciousness (the true essence of who we are) manifest our true purpose and potential in this world. But all too often, instead of the database using language and our thoughts to help us manifest our true potential, our own thoughts become a double-edged sword. Let us take a closer look at how this incredible tool of language, which arguably has been one of our strongest assets as a species, can often turn on us.

Understanding How Language Empowers The Database

What happens to the relationship between our unique consciousness and the database as language develops further?

During our earliest years, our unique consciousness is the dominant force in our life and the place from which we draw our sense of self. While the database of our mind is rapidly acquiring information and forming mental models, it is relatively "empty" when we first begin life. All this dramatically changes when we develop language. With language, there is not only an explosion in the amount of information in the database, but language also enables our mind to start creating beliefs and forming thoughts about ourselves and our environment at an incredibly rapid rate in order to help us successfully navigate the world. Our mind loves to think and when language really comes on board, it is off to the races. While it's obviously a tremendous asset that our mind is able to use language to think so effectively, all too often an unfortunate thing happens as the database increases in size. As it goes through this incredible growth spurt, its weight starts shifting the balance of our focus from our unique consciousness toward the database. We start getting pulled farther and farther into the database and farther from our unique consciousness (the true essence of who we are).

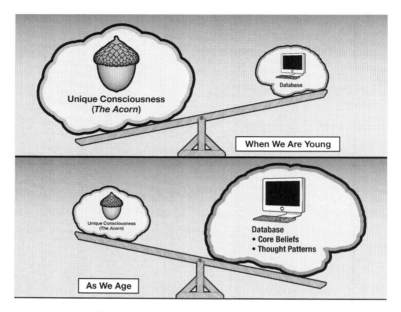

FIGURE 5: How the balance shifts from the
unique consciousness to our database

How do we start losing sight of who we really are and get trapped by the database?

The reason we get drawn farther and farther into the database has to do with the power we give to language. Our thoughts and beliefs are merely words that reflect the data our mind has collected from our experiences and subsequent interpretations. The real problem occurs when instead of realizing that our thoughts merely reflect all our experiences and the dysfunction we were exposed to, we start believing the thoughts in our heads as if they were absolute truth (Hayes, 2005).

As our beliefs and thought patterns become more solidified, that voice in our head, that internal dialogue we all have with ourselves, starts to become louder and more and more dominant. This voice begins to speak in such a confident, commanding tone that most of us fall into the trap of blindly accepting what it says as absolute truth—we never even think to question it. So if that voice tells us "I'm not good enough," "I can't do that," or "They won't like me," guess what? We absolutely believe what it's saying as a foregone conclusion, a done deal. We lose sight of the fact that if we had been raised in a different environment, we would most likely have a very different set of core beliefs about ourselves, others and the world. Yet we would still be fundamentally the same person—our unique consciousness would not have changed. The only thing that would have changed was the programming of the database of our mind.

As the thoughts and beliefs in the database become more and more dominant, the sad reality is that many of us lose sight of the unique consciousness we entered the world with—the real essence of who we are. We start letting the words of the database define who we are, whether we are lovable, worthwhile, intelligent, etc., and what we are capable of doing or not. Think about how ironic that is—the database, which was really not even there (or at least had relatively little information in it) when our unique consciousness entered the world (when YOU entered the world), has the audacity to think it knows exactly who you are and can sum you up using a few words or core beliefs. And the sad thing is we believe it!

As soon as we start blindly believing what the database has to say about ourselves, our capabilities and the world around us, we are trapped. The power over deciding how we approach life has shifted almost entirely from our unique consciousness to the database of our mind. The database that was always supposed to be a tool to help us manifest our unique consciousness and our purpose in the world now becomes our master. It then proceeds to put us on a wild-goose chase of defining our worth and value based on its criteria and telling us what we "should" do in order to be "happy" in this world. While it's doing this, we are getting further and further away from our unique consciousness, which is the only place where true happiness can be found.

FIGURE 6: The prison cell of beliefs

If the unique consciousness is such a source of wisdom, why does it get so overshadowed by the database?

The reason the database becomes such a dominant force in our lives is once again because of the power we give to verbal language (Hayes, 2005). Instead of seeing our ability to use words to create our thoughts as an incredible tool for us to navigate and construct our lives, we start believing our thoughts blindly, as if they were absolute truth, and letting them define who we are. The database ends up becoming dominant over the "voice" of the unique consciousness because the unique consciousness doesn't speak in words or language, per se. Instead, the unique consciousness "speaks" in energy shifts in the body (things we are drawn toward versus things we steer away from), our gut feelings, our intuition, and our deep emotional reactions to things that really resonate with us. It also speaks in images, dreams, visions we have for our future, and our natural talents and abilities. Sadly, because we are so often preoccupied listening to the words and thoughts of the database, we frequently don't hear the "voice" of the unique consciousness. At other times, we may hear the "voice," but it gets trumped by whatever the database is saying. Now remember, the database is full of programming largely acquired from our childhood, so it reflects the views, teachings and dysfunction of our parents, relatives, teachers, coaches, friends, society, media and culture. The unique consciousness, on the other hand is organic—no one "programmed" the acorn. Our unique consciousness was determined by whatever energy, force or higher power brought us into this world.

Take a moment to think about what we give up when we choose to let the voice of the database dominate our life. Not only do we lose touch with who we really are and our true purpose in this world, but as we will see in the next section, life from within the database looks and feels entirely different from life where we remain grounded in our unique consciousness. Let us now take a look at how these experiences differ so greatly.

Understanding How It Feels To Be Trapped In Your Database

In order to be in a position to truly grow beyond your mind, you need to understand how differently life looks and feels from the perspective of our unique consciousness (who we really are) versus the database (the collection of what we've learned from our experiences). Another term you may have heard that is often used to describe the database is "ego." Living life trapped within the ego/database feels entirely different from when we are able to stay grounded in our unique consciousness and utilize the database as a tool, as it was originally intended.

Life from within the ego/database ends up feeling like a job—a perpetual struggle to find meaning and purpose in your life, a "rat race" where you're chasing happiness but never actually reach it. When you're caught up in your ego, you define your self-worth based on your achievements, things you've accumulated, appearances or how you compare to others. You frequently experience feelings of stress, anxiety, feeling down or a sense of emptiness inside that you may try to fill with things external to yourself like food, possessions and distractions. You may experience an overall dissatisfaction with your life (particularly with your career or relationships) and feel like you're living life reactively—just responding to current stressors or demands, but not making any true progress. Last, but sometimes most significantly, you feel like fears and doubts frequently hold you back from what you're really meant to do in this life.

On the other hand, when we're able to remain grounded in our unique consciousness and maintain the perspective of utilizing the database as a tool to help us manifest our true purpose and potential, life looks and feels entirely different. When you're able to go through life staying connected to your unique consciousness, you end up having a solid sense of who you are and feeling like you have inherent, unconditional worth and value. You never feel threatened by other people's talents or accomplishments but instead have deep, meaningful relationships and connections with other people. You experience positive energy and excitement about life and feel like you're continually growing and developing as a person. You feel like you're doing what you were meant to do in life and that you're making a positive impact on other people's lives and the world in general. Ultimately, you feel fully engaged in life and believe that your life has a deep sense of meaning and purpose.

Think about how we go through our lives as a wide spectrum: at one end is our unique consciousness (a place where we're able to stay fully grounded in our true selves and utilize our database and body as tools to manifest our genuine purpose) and at the other end is the ego/database (a place where we are fully trapped by the words of our ego/database and have lost sight entirely of who we really are). People fall at all points along this spectrum in terms of how connected they are to their true selves versus how trapped they are by their ego/database. There are people in our world today who have been able to connect with their true selves and free themselves almost entirely from their ego/database. On the other hand, there are many people who are so trapped by their ego/database and let it define who they are to such an extent that they hardly ever have even a moment of peace in this world. Following the pattern of the normal bell curve, the majority of people fall at all different points in between.

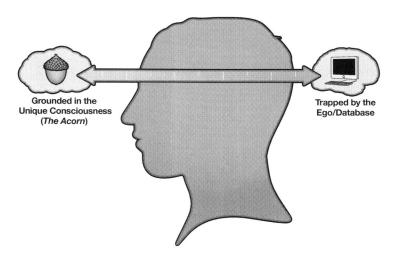

Grounded in the
Unique Consciousness
(*The Acorn*)

Trapped by the
Ego/Database

FIGURE 7: From being grounded in the "acorn" to trapped by the ego

How the unique consciousness and the ego/database differ on three key questions.

One of the reasons life feels so very different from the place of the unique consciousness versus the ego/database is because these perspectives resolve three key questions, which are fundamental to all human beings, very differently:

Who am I, and do I have self-worth?

How do I have relationships?
How can I be truly content in this world?

Let us now take a closer look at how our unique consciousness and the ego/database differ in their responses to these important questions.

Key Question #1:
Who am I, and do I have self-worth?

The question of "Who am I?" and the subsequent question—"Do I have self-worth?"—are two of the most fundamental questions we as human beings need to resolve to be truly content in this world. Let's see what both the ego/database and the unique consciousness have to say in response.

Ego/database: According to the ego/database, who you are and your self-worth are conditional/dependent upon either something external to yourself or how you compare to others. The ego/database can choose almost anything external to you to base your worth on, such as intelligence, academic or athletic performance, musical/artistic talent, income level, status, popularity, attractiveness or your jean size. The other favorite choice for the ego in terms of deciding who you are and your worth is how you compare to others. Therefore, your sense of self-worth would depend upon whether or not you felt you were smarter, more attractive, more successful or more talented than those people around you.

There are obvious major drawbacks to accepting the ego's conditional definition of who we are and our worth. One is that it breeds almost perpetual anxiety and insecurity. Think about the ego/database's sense of you as like a house of cards—everything may be fine for the moment if every card stays exactly in place. But heaven forbid one of the cards falls: then it feels like the whole thing could come tumbling down. That's the sense of fragility you would feel if you were firmly trapped in your ego/database. The ego puts you on a wild-goose chase of finding the "magic key" to eventually finally being "good enough." But even if you achieve one of the criteria the ego sets out before you (e.g., you reach a certain income level, get a certain GPA, finally fit into certain jeans or get invited to a popular party), you cannot rest too long because the ego works on the "what have you done for me lately" mentality.

To understand how the ego works, imagine you have a big old wooden barrel and you get a huge influx of water (maybe you get a promotion, make your numbers for the quarter or buy a bigger home). You may feel "filled" or "good enough" for the moment. But then the reality hits that there are little holes in the bottom of the barrel and the water level starts dissipating relatively quickly. You find you need another "hit," such as more money or a vacation home, in order to maintain your level of self-worth. Unfortunately, you fall into a pattern similar to any addiction—needing more and more to achieve a "hit" of self-esteem but never really being truly satisfied. It's never enough. You never really reach this "good enough" status that the ego is trying to sell. You may have momentary glimpses of it, but these moments never last too long.

The other major drawback comes from when the ego tells you that who you are and your worth is based on how you compare to others. When you fall into this trap, you are frequently motivated to either artificially inflate yourself above others or to take others down in order to ensure that your "stock value" remains relatively high. Very likely you can recall a time when you may have met someone and they made sure to let you know (subtly or not-so-subtly) that they were either smarter, more educated or made more money than you did. Think back to how it felt speaking with that person—did it feel even remotely genuine? Probably not; sadly, that's how the ego talks and tries to interact with people.

The implications of the ego's conditional sense of worth go far beyond just making our interactions with others feel "fake" or contrived. The insecurity it breeds is largely responsible for most, if not all, of the aggressive (both passive and direct) and amoral behavior in the world. Frequently, the ego becomes so tenacious in its desire to feed itself in order to maintain a sense of self-worth that it trumps any sense of compassion or consideration for others. You may see relentless pursuits of external markers of success with little or no regard for consequences to others or their well-being. The ego may also "take others down" by passing judgments, criticizing, ostracizing or bullying—all in an attempt to artificially boost its self-esteem. As insecurity rises, so does vicious behavior. For example, the reason junior high school can be such a difficult time for people (especially with girls being vicious to each other) is that it's often the height of insecurity, with the onset of puberty and social changes. Junior high school is often the time of life where the ego has the greatest hold on our sense of self. While many grow out of this insecurity as they develop a deeper sense of self and greater self-acceptance with age, many stay trapped in their ego and insecurities their whole lives and perpetuate such negative behavior into adulthood.

Unique Consciousness: The unique consciousness, on the other hand, answers the question of who you are and whether you have worth very differently than the ego/database does. The unique consciousness knows that your self-worth is unconditional and inherent in the fact that you are a unique human being. There are billions of people in this world but there is no other YOU any-where. You have come into this world with a unique set of poten-tials that only you could bring. You have a unique purpose to fulfill that only you can. Once you fully comprehend these points, you realize that you do not have to be threatened by anyone else in the world—who out there could be a better YOU than you? You've got dibs on the job—you've got the monopoly on being YOU. So the first part of the equation is realizing, "I don't have to worry about anyone else being a better me than me." Once you really under-stand this concept, how much time do you recommend I spend trying to be a better YOU than you (or better anyone else, for that matter)? Sadly, this is exactly what people trapped in the ego/data-base do all the time. They spend their lives trying to be like some-one else, thinking that's going to increase their self-worth. It's like the little oak seedling spending all its time and energy trying to be like the nearby maples and pines. That would be foolish, yet that's exactly what the ego/database encourages.

When you are able to stay grounded in your unique conscious-ness and realize that you have unconditional worth, you are no longer motivated to artificially put yourself above or below anyone else, nor are you driven in any way, shape or form to "take them down." You simply want to be yourself to your fullest potential and you want others to be themselves to the greatest extent possible as well. As long as when they're being themselves, they don't impact your ability to be YOU, you're able to give them your blessing to be who they are, free from your judgment or any desire to control or unduly influence them. The only time you would really have issues with other people is if they are in some way, shape or form inhibiting you from being YOU to your fullest (either by trying to control you or making it harder for you to reach your potential in some way). In such cases, all you would be motivated to do is defend your boundary of YOU—you still would not be motivated to take the other person down, you would just want them to back off (respect your boundary) and give you the space and freedom you need.

To understand the perspective of the unique consciousness when it comes to your self-worth, think about a puzzle. With a puzzle, each piece has a unique part to play that only it can, the same way that you bring a unique constellation of potentials (natural abilities, talents and passions) that only you can bring. Now, the thing to realize is that the puzzle only works when each piece is present and plays its part. Doesn't it bother you if, when you're piecing together a puzzle, you end up missing any of the pieces? It doesn't matter if it's a basic solid piece or the most elaborately designed one—the puzzle is not complete until all the pieces are in place. Also, have you ever been working on a puzzle and you think a piece fits into a certain location, so you force it a bit, but it really belongs someplace else? Most of the time when you do this you end up damaging the piece and confusing the puzzle. People are the same way. How many people do you think are trying to fill a piece of the puzzle they really weren't meant to fill because the ego/database told them they should?

Unlike the ego/database, the unique consciousness answers the question of who you are, not based on what it thinks you should be, but on what's in your acorn—the unique set of potentials with which you entered the world. From the place of the unique consciousness, you realize that even though you are here on earth, you came from and are able to maintain a connection with a larger energy force, be it God, a higher power, or a universal energy. This energy is driving you to develop your potentials and fulfill your part or purpose in this world. It is what gives us human beings our natural inclination to grow and develop our talents and abilities. From the perspective of the unique consciousness, it's not only our unique talents and abilities but also those things that resonate most deeply with us—our core values, passions, dreams and ideas we are capable of creating or conceiving—that help us understand who we really are and what we are really meant to do. The key is to learn how to both discover and then develop what's really at our core. But before discussing how to do this further, let us turn to our next fundamental question.

Key Question #2: How do I have relationships?

As humans beings, we enter this world with an inborn attachment system that motivates us to try and form an emotional bond with our caregivers. While we have this natural instinct to try and emotionally connect with others, we are not born knowing how to form healthy relationships, per se. Instead, we learn how to establish relationships based on our experiences and what we've been taught. As you will see below, the models of how to form relationships differ significantly from the perspective of the ego/database versus that of the unique consciousness.

Ego/database: Think about the ego/database's approach to relationships as similar to how teenagers might manage their image on Facebook. According to the ego, in order to have "successful" relationships, you need to look a certain way, act a certain way, be interested in certain things and be willing to do things to make other people happy so they will want to be in a relationship with you. Often this ideal of who you are "supposed to be" and what you are "supposed to do" is established by your friends, family, society and culture, rather than being based on who you really are and what's most meaningful for you. Because the ego is so concerned with how you compare to other people and external markers of success, relationships tend to involve a great deal of control, manipulation, power differentials and "games" that people play. Also, they typically only reach a relatively shallow level of emotional depth because you're either not being who you really are or you end up being unwilling to make yourself emotionally vulnerable to others because it's too risky.

Unique consciousness: From the perspective of the unique consciousness, on the other hand, you are more comfortable and secure with who you are and are able to first connect with yourself on a much deeper level than could ever be possible from the ego/database. When you form a relationship, you are able to just be yourself and you want the other person to just be who they are as well. When people are just being themselves, there are going to be times when certain people feel more chemistry, an emotional connection or that the other person just "gets them"—be it in a friendship, at work or in a romantic situation, and subsequently a relationship just naturally develops. From the place of the unique consciousness, when you're in a relationship, you're not looking to control, dominate or manipulate the other person in any way. Instead, you are just looking to share who you are and your life with them and looking for them to do the same. If the emotional connection between you deepens, you develop a sense of mutual trust, respect and possibly love for each other. You try to be open, honest and respectful in your communication and when conflict does occur, you try to handle it in an emotionally mature way.

It may seem a bit ironic, but one of the examples I like to use to understand the very basic model of healthy relationships is observing groups of toddlers in daycare. One of the things I love most about toddler age is that toddlers are often able to just be themselves to the fullest. They haven't reached the age when kids become more self-conscious and start censoring how they act. If you observe a classroom of toddlers, you will already be able to see many elements of who they really are—their different personalities, interests and ways of doing things. You may see some children going up and down the slide repeatedly, others sitting quietly playing in the sandbox, or still others exploring and looking for caterpillars. But one thing you will also see is that certain children will just naturally gravitate toward other particular children. They will have their "buddies" that they will seek to spend more time playing with, and it is not uncommon to see certain toddlers holding hands with each other. Ironically, it's only when they get older and the ego/database starts telling them how to have relationships that things start getting complicated.

Now let us take a look at the last fundamental question that all human beings grapple with at some point in their lives.

Key Question #3: How can I be truly content in this world?

As human beings, we are not only looking to have a healthy sense of who we are and relationships with others. We are also ultimately looking to find true contentment and happiness in this world. Sadly, for those deeply and perpetually trapped in the ego/database, true, genuine, enduring happiness will elude them until they find a way of freeing themselves.

Ego/database: For those trapped in the ego/database, the ego will send you on a wild-goose chase trying to convince you that if you achieve certain things, look a certain way, or do what you are supposed to do to be "successful," you will ultimately be happy. While those things may give you fleeting moments of happiness, they will never bring you true contentment. The reason that you can never find true contentment from the perspective of the ego/database goes back to the fact that when you are trapped in your ego, you aren't able to see who you truly are and develop a healthy sense of self. This healthy sense of self is really the key prerequisite to true contentment. The way I like to describe it is if you were baking a cake, it's the flour of the cake. So many people out there who are trapped in the ego are trying to bake a cake without this "flour." Instead, they're focusing on piling on the frosting and the decorations and are confused as to why it's not working. They experience fleeting glimpses of joy and contentment, only to have them fade and leave them seeking more "frosting" or "decorations" (anything external to themselves, such as material items, accomplishments, prestige or body image). You'll never be able to make the cake without the flour, no matter how many layers of frosting or how elaborate the decorations, but that's exactly what the ego would have you believe. The flour is the key ingredient and it is found by connecting with the unique consciousness, not in chasing frosting and decorations.

Unique consciousness: Unlike the ego, the unique consciousness knows the path to true, lasting contentment. In order to be truly content in this world, you must first learn how to free yourself from the ego/database (we will be talking more about how to do this in the next section). The next step is to figure out what's in your acorn. What I mean by this is to start knowing yourself at a deep enough level to discover what talents, natural abilities and passions are within you at your core (we will also be talking about strategies for doing this in step nine). Once you start discovering what you were meant to do, you need to find the right "soil" in which to develop your acorn. By "soil," I mean finding whatever resources or experiences you need (education, training or mentoring) that would help you develop your talents, strengths and passions. The final step toward true contentment is that once you have discovered and developed your gifts, you must find a way to use them to make a positive impact on something beyond yourself: other people, animals, the environment or by contributing to a body of knowledge.

Therefore, finding true contentment all begins with learning to free yourself from the ego/database and living life more and more from the perspective of the unique consciousness. Let us now begin examining how to do just that—break free from the ego and reunite with your unique consciousness, or who you really are.

Phase Two

....

Discovering
the Real You

Learning To Live
Outside The Database

As long as you allow yourself to be continually trapped by the beliefs and programming of the database, true contentment will elude you. In order to experience true freedom, you must learn to free yourself from your database and live life more grounded in your unique consciousness. There are two keys to freeing yourself from your database. The first is learning to stop giving words so much power and then to become an observer. Let us begin with the issue of how words end up trapping us.

How do I stop giving words so much power?

In Step 6, we learned how the ego/database uses words to form core beliefs and our thoughts. We saw how so many of us have the tendency to get trapped by allowing the beliefs of the database to start defining us and what we are or are not capable of doing. In essence, we allow the database to imprison us in a cell of words and beliefs because we believe the words to be absolute truth and lose sight of what words really are. We give words the same power to imprison us as if we were actually completely surrounded by steel bars with no way out. We forget that words are merely symbols—a tool we as a species have developed to help us communicate. Think about this example for a moment: if I was sitting in front of you with a white poster board and wrote the words "grizzly bear" on it, would you be scared? If I even held up a picture of a grizzly bear, would you be scared? Of course not. You wouldn't be scared because you would be able to keep the perspective that a word and a picture of a grizzly bear present no real danger to you. You could differentiate the experience of seeing a word (a symbol) and a picture (another symbol) from the experience of being in the presence of a real grizzly bear that would actually pose a threat to you. What's important to understand about our thoughts, however, is that when a thought or belief (which are merely strings of words) goes across our consciousness, our mind is often not able to keep the same perspective. We react to our thoughts as if what we are thinking is actually happening. We end up reacting as if there were an actual grizzly bear right in front of us (Hayes, 2005).

The other problem we have with our beliefs and thoughts is that we tend not to question them, but to blindly accept them as absolute truth. Our beliefs and thoughts have power over us only because we believe them. It is similar to what happened in the *Wizard of Oz*—the wizard only had power because Dorothy and her cohort believed he did. Our words (and the beliefs and thoughts we construct with them) are the same way—they only have power to the extent that we believe them and accept them as absolute truth.

If you want to free yourself from your ego/database, you must start understanding that the beliefs and thoughts in your database did not come down from on high on stone tablets. They are far from absolute truth; rather, they are beliefs and habits in thinking that reflect the relative health or dysfunction of our parents, relatives, friends, teachers, coaches, society, media and culture. I would encourage you to stop blindly accepting what the ego/database is selling you. Instead, start looking at your beliefs and thoughts as proposals that your ego/database is offering you. If you are at work and someone hands you a proposal for a project, what do you do with it? Do you blindly accept it without even reading it? Hopefully not. Instead, you look at it, read it over and decide whether or not you agree with it. You may endorse some of it and want to edit other parts of it, or you may reject the whole proposal. The key is to start learning to examine your thoughts and beliefs and to look at them as proposals that require your endorsement—or not.

The first step in this process is to really understand that words only have power to the extent we listen to and believe them. At no point in time can a symbol (a word or a string of words) actually handcuff you or prevent you from taking action unless you give it that power. Start seeing your thoughts and beliefs as merely a collection of symbols. Start realizing that the wizard was really just a little man with a megaphone.

Understanding the ego's biggest weapons: fear and doubt

Now the other tricky thing you need to understand about the ego/database is that once it has you trapped, it really has no interest in letting you go. It seems to have a way of feeding on the power and control it has over your life and has no interest in graciously encouraging or allowing you to freely connect with your unique consciousness. Instead, if the ego feels like you're starting to try to take a step back and free yourself from it or if it thinks you're onto the fact that it doesn't actually have any real power (but just smokescreens and illusions), the ego will pull out all the stops to keep you within its grasp. Two of the ego's favorite "weapons" are fear and doubt, with a close third being guilt. When someone is first trying to loosen the grip the ego has on them, often what happens is that the ego may use thoughts like "I can't do it," "It won't work," or one of its favorite phrases, "What if…" So frequently what happens is that you take a step or two toward the unique consciousness, and that triggers the ego to turn the volume up on fear, doubt, and/or guilt, and the next thing you know you're back in the ego's trap. The ego wants to remain in control of your life and when it doesn't get its way (i.e., you start realizing you don't have to listen to it), it is not beyond the ego to throw a "tantrum" where it speaks more and more loudly, with such assertiveness and authority that you comply.

But again, the key to remember is that the ego has no real power. The only power it has is that which we give to it by believing what it says. Stop blindly believing what it says and the ego crumbles like a house of cards. Once you fundamentally understand that no matter what the ego says, no matter how loudly it says it and with what authority it speaks—no matter what, *you don't have to listen* to it—then you will have taken a huge step toward true freedom and being able to reconnect with your unique consciousness.

Becoming the observer

Once you stop giving the words of the ego/database so much power, the other key step toward true freedom is getting into the role of an "observer" of the ego/database. What I mean by observer is that instead of going through life trapped inside the database, imagine taking a step back where you can get more of a bird's-eye view of the database and start watching the thoughts and ideas that go across your consciousness. Frequently we pay little to no attention to our thoughts; they happen so quickly and automatically that instead we just react to them like pinballs inside a pinball machine. When you become the observer, you bring your conscious awareness or attention to your thoughts—you start watching your thoughts (Kabat-Zinn, 1994). Start by asking yourself, "What is my mind doing?" "What is it I'm thinking?" Imagine your database as a factory that is producing thoughts. Start looking at the "products" (thoughts) coming out of the assembly line. The mere act of bringing your conscious awareness toward your thoughts helps you take a step out of the database toward the role of observer—a step closer to your unique consciousness.

How do I take a passive attitude toward my thoughts?

One of the keys to getting into the role of observer is learning to have a passive attitude toward your thoughts (Benson, 2000). What I mean by passive attitude is that as a thought goes across your consciousness, you first *label* it for what it is—a thought. Then, as best you can, just let the thought come into your consciousness and go out of your consciousness without "grabbing" it. Let it just naturally flow down your "stream" of consciousness. To help clarify what I mean by a passive attitude, consider the following example: if I was sitting still trying to ground myself in the observer role, I might notice the thought, "I have to go to the grocery store." I first label it, saying to myself "There's the *thought* I have to go to grocery store." As best I can, I would let that thought come in and go out of my consciousness without engaging it. What if, on the other hand, the thought, "I have to go to the grocery store" comes into my consciousness and I starting thinking "What do I need at the grocery store?" and "What are we having for dinner?" Do you see how I "grabbed" the thought and then my mind was off to the races? Learning that you don't have to engage a thought simply because your mind produces it is fundamental to getting into the observer role and ultimately freeing yourself from the ego/database.

Some metaphors to help you get into the observer role

When working with clients, I have found it helpful to use imagery and metaphors to help people understand and access the observer role more easily.

The riverbank

For the first metaphor, picture a large, rushing river with waves and even some whitewater coming down the river. The river represents the contents of your mind—your thoughts, feelings, memories, behavioral impulses, etc. (the whitewater being the negative thoughts and stronger emotions). Now imagine you're right in the middle of the river getting pelted by the negative thoughts or feelings. How's that feel? If you're like most, the answer is "not good" or "overwhelming."

Avoidance strategies

When we feel like we're smack in the middle of the river, on the verge of being knocked over, our natural tendency is to try and start holding back or "filtering" the river. Picture trying to hold back a river with your two bare hands and you can get a sense of how much energy/effort might be involved in attempting to do this. The way our mind attempts to "hold back" the river is with a variety of what we call avoidance strategies. An avoidance strategy involves any obsessive or compulsive behavior that occupies or numbs our mind in an attempt to prevent it from fully experiencing what is upsetting it. Some of the most popular avoidance strategies in our society include workaholism; perfectionism; body image/eating issues; alcoholism; being obsessed with money, fame, status, prestige, or material items; constantly needing to be doing something (watching TV, surfing the net, etc.) or any substance abuse. Take a look around and ask yourself how pervasive are the use of avoidance strategies in our society?

Now people may ask what's so wrong with using these avoidance strategies? To be honest, avoidance strategies, used sparingly, aren't necessarily a bad thing. The problem is that, all too often, the avoidance strategies don't stay at this level, but instead take on a life of their own and end up controlling us, rather than the other way around. The other downside is that the *river* (our thoughts, feelings, behavioral impulses, etc.) is a rich source of information for us to understand ourselves more deeply, as well as what might be coming up for us at any point in time. Having uncensored access to this information would put us in a much better position to navigate life.

So how do we obtain this "uncensored access?" We need to get into the observer role. In order to do this, imagine the exact same river with the same whitewater and large waves, but now see yourself on a nice, secure, high bank—well above the water level. When you're on the bank, you can stay perfectly still, even if the river is rushing. From this perspective, you can safely observe the river with no danger of being swept away by it. You can now just let the river flow freely, observing it as it goes by.

Even if the river contains intense feelings like anger, fear, anxiety, guilt or painful negative thoughts such as "I'm worthless" or "I'll never succeed," it is "safe" to allow these thoughts and emotions to come up from the vantage point of the riverbank—unlike when you're smack in the middle of the river. So first imagine removing yourself from the river (literally pulling yourself out of the current) then sitting still on the riverbank as you watch the river and the waves flowing past you. Start watching the river and ask yourself, "What is my mind doing?" or "What's coming up for me?" or "What's being triggered?" Then use the strategy of labeling what you observe, be it a thought, memory, emotion or behavioral impulse. For example, instead of saying "I'm worthless," say "There's the thought that I'm worthless" or instead of "I'm anxious," say "There's the feeling of anxiety." Many people find the combination of imagery and the technique of verbally describing and labeling, *without judging* what's in the "river," to be very effective in helping them get into the observer role.

The coach's box

Another metaphor that I find effective for not only getting into the observer role but also helping us learn how to respond rather than react to situations is that of a coach's box. For those of you familiar with football, imagine you are a defensive lineman (for those not familiar with football, these are the guys who stand right on the line of scrimmage) and you have the offensive lineman literally right smack in your face on the other side of the line of scrimmage. As the defensive lineman, your primary job is to react to the offensive guy right in front of you, trying to block or deflect his actions. Now imagine the offensive lineman is really the contents of your mind or database—your thoughts, feelings, memories and behavioral impulses—and all you do is react to whatever is coming up in your mind. So in essence, you end up being at the mercy of whatever neuron or neural pathway in the database is being triggered at any point in time.

Next consider the same scenario of a football game but this time, instead of being on the field as the lineman, imagine you are up in the coach's box (the box way above the stands where some coaches sit during the game). The reason some coaches sit up in the coach's box is that they can get an aerial perspective of the whole field, a much broader, more comprehensive perspective than they could ever get from the sidelines. From the coach's box, a coach can get a better understanding of what the other team is doing (or what his own team is doing, for that matter) and then—and this is the key—he can *think about* what adjustments his team needs to make or how his team can *respond* rather than *react*.

How do I learn how to respond rather than react?

Now the difference between reacting versus responding is crucial. Reacting doesn't allow any time to think. It's what happens in a pinball machine—a stimulus and a quick reaction. When you're *responding*, you get this little window of time (you don't typically need that much time; often a few seconds will do) where you see what's going on (or what's coming up for you) and you *think* about what you want to do or what would be the best way to *respond* to the situation. Take a moment and think about how many situations in your life might have gone very differently if you had only had a few extra moments to calm down or think through a situation before you acted. The more you grasp the information and practice the techniques presented here, the more effectively you will be able to do exactly that for yourself.

Meditation and other centering techniques

When I talk about getting into the "observer" role and learning to watch your own mind, what I'm actually encouraging you to practice is a form of mindfulness meditation. Broadly speaking, mindfulness meditation can be defined as learning to become a non-judgmental observer of your own mind (Kabat-Zinn, 1994). In addition to learning to take a passive attitude toward your thoughts, meditation involves being able to train and direct your focus of attention and conscious awareness. Ultimately, all meditation and other centering techniques such as yoga, tai chi, qigong and chanting help to free you from the database and bring you closer to the place of your unique consciousness. The more you practice meditation or other centering techniques, the easier it is for you to reach a place of stillness, quiet and peace—a place free of the thoughts of your database, a place where you can connect more deeply with your unique consciousness and "listen" to how it is trying to guide you in your life.

There are many different forms of meditation and techniques for helping you bring about a meditative state. Some of these techniques involve focusing your attention on your breathing, using mantras, prayers or chanting, or using meditative sounds or movements. There are many excellent resources that I mention on the website for learning about and exploring different meditation and centering techniques. I would encourage you to take the time to explore a variety of these techniques for yourself. Finding a technique that you not only feel comfortable with and is effective for you, but one you are also willing to incorporate into your daily life will be very important in freeing yourself from your mind and helping you reconnect with your unique consciousness. The more you connect with your unique consciousness, the deeper your awareness of who you truly are, along with a better understanding of your purpose in this world.

Let us now turn to the next section, where we learn how to listen more deeply to the unique consciousness within us.

Understanding How To Listen To The Unique Consciousness

When I talk about learning to "listen" to and understand your unique consciousness (the true essence of who you are that was there the day you were born), I often say let's help you figure out "What's in your acorn?" Just as an acorn contains the full potential of an oak tree, an infant baby contains the full potential of who he or she may become some day. When I talk about figuring out "what's in your acorn," I mean to start discovering that unique set of potentials—the "seeds" of your strengths, interests, passions, personality traits and ways your mind can work—that you brought into this world the day you were born. The more you discover the set of potentials you came into this world with, the more your true purpose in this world will be revealed. So many people spend so much time and effort trying to figure out what they *should* do, but the more you understand who you really are, the more you will understand what you are really *meant* to do.

The "voice" of the unique consciousness

Unfortunately, the sad reality is that many people go through their whole lives without ever really knowing their true selves—even though we hang out with ourselves every moment we're alive.

The reason our true selves often stay hidden is that the "voice" of the unique consciousness is often overshadowed by that of the ego/database. Where the ego/database speaks in words, the unique consciousness speaks in our "gut" feelings, intuition, energy shifts in our body (things we are drawn toward versus away from), emotions, imagery, dreams, ways our mind naturally works and personality traits. Many times people are so preoccupied with the chatter of the database that they don't even hear the unique consciousness talking. Other times, people may hear their gut saying one thing but they let that voice be trumped by what the database is saying they "should" do.

Now, the reason it's so important to learn to listen and trust the voice of the unique consciousness is that it is the best source of information for who you truly are and what your real purpose was meant to be in this world. Let me explain. Remember, the database contains the programming of everything we have been taught, observed or have made interpretations about, beginning from our earliest caregivers and family members all the way through our exposure to commercials, TV shows and our culture in general. It's greatly influenced by other people's ideas and opinions—and their dysfunction. It's not uncommon for many of us to hear comments from those surrounding us about who we are, what we're capable or incapable of doing, or what we "should" or should not do. All those voices get incorporated into the programming of our database, much of the time without us even being consciously aware of it. But the thing about the unique consciousness is that no one has programmed it. The unique consciousness enters the world "preprogrammed," just like an acorn comes into the world preprogrammed to be an oak tree. Whatever life force you believe brings a baby into existence—be it God, the universe or a biological life force—is responsible for the "programming" of the unique consciousness. It's therefore not influenced by other people (along with their insecurities and dysfunction) and our surroundings the same way our database is. The result is that the unique consciousness is a "purer," more organic source of information concerning who we are and what we were really designed to do in this world than our database ever could be. That's why it's so important to learn to listen to and trust this incredible source of information: it's your best guide to finding true contentment. The ego/database only sends you on a wild-goose chase, convincing you it knows the way to make you really happy, but only ever delivering fleeting moments of fun, excitement or happiness—never true, enduring contentment.

So how do you learn to listen to the unique consciousness?

"Close your eyes so you can start seeing.
Cover your ears so you can start hearing."

I like this quote because it brings your attention to the mistake many people make in trying to learn about themselves—namely, looking in the wrong direction. Many people look to their environment, comparing themselves to others or to external markers of success when trying to figure out who they are. Instead of looking outward, the key to learning about your true self, the unique consciousness, is to turn your attention inward. Below are several strategies to help you learn to do just that.

Listen to your body

Our bodies are a tremendous source of information about the unique consciousness that many of us don't remotely tap into as fully as we could. When you're engaging in certain activities or even just imagining doing so, draw your awareness and attention to how your body feels. Do you feel lighter, more positive energy going through you, or does even thinking about doing that particular activity feel like a weight on your shoulders? Is it something you just feel drawn to or do you have the opposite reaction? Those energy shifts in your body can be very informative in helping you discover what you're meant to do. For example, I once had a client who had the opportunity to work for a year in Singapore, and his body language clearly indicated how excited he was at the opportunity. Noticing his body language, I reflected back to him that there was an adventurous spirit to who he inherently was. He looked at me, a little perplexed, and asked, "Wouldn't everyone jump at that opportunity?" Meanwhile, as he was telling me about the opportunity, I was having a visceral reaction like, "There's no way I would live for a year in Singapore." I'm definitely someone who's more adventurous with ideas than with living long term in a foreign land. Fortunately for this client, his job allowed him to travel around the world and was a good match for his adventurous spirit. If, on the other hand, he had been in a career that did not allow any travel or exploring of different cultures, he would likely have felt stifled and experienced some level of angst or agitation. That's how it feels when you're trying to do something that's not a good match for your "acorn." I would feel something similar if I had a job where I had to travel all the time or be away from my home for extended periods of time, whereas I'm very content with a career that does not involve much travel but allows me the opportunity to explore ideas and different philosophies and approaches. The key concept to understand is that when something is a good match for your "acorn," you will experience feelings of excitement and positive energy. When it's not, you will either feel no significant reaction (a "whatever" kind of feeling) or a weight or negative reaction in your body. Just learning to listen to these energy shifts in your body can greatly increase your ability to navigate life in ways that are more in line with who you really are.

Watch the nonverbal activity of your mind

When you're trying to learn more about your unique consciousness, an important skill to develop is learning to observe the nonverbal activity of your mind. What I mean by the nonverbal activity is images that come to your mind—dreams, things you can just "see," or ideas for inventions or solutions that pop into your mind, as in moments of epiphany. Also, watch what your mind naturally does in certain situations. For instance, I've had clients who can just walk into a room and see how it might be redecorated or who think it's a game to bargain shop for outfits where everything coordinates to a "T," from their earrings down to their shoes. Other people may walk into the same room and be totally oblivious to the décor or choose being comfortable or practical rather than making sure everything in their outfit is coordinated. I know other people whose minds think it's a "game" to try and figure out how the chef made a particular dish when eating at a restaurant, while their partners are just content to simply enjoy the dish with no thought to how it was made. Some people, when looking at a particular product or how a company does business, automatically see ways the product can be improved or more effective strategies the company might use. I've known people who thought it was fun solving biochemistry equations or programming a computer, while both those activities would make my head hurt. The ideas that just flow to your mind naturally and those activities it has fun playing with are important clues as to what you are most ideally designed to do.

Discover your strengths and weaknesses

One of the unfortunate things I've noticed in working with people is that often their strongest talents or skills are the ones they overlook. Because people's strengths come so naturally to them and involve relatively little effort, many people assume that everyone must be able to do the same thing or think in the same way. Sadly, those talents are often viewed as "no big deal" rather than the gifts they actually are. I've seen people devalue talents like being able to speak multiple languages, learn a musical instrument by themselves, solve complex math equations, write eloquently, solve problems creatively and remain composed under pressure. There have been many times I've pointed out strengths to clients, only to have them be confused that not everyone was able to do what they could. Learning about your relative strengths and weaknesses is one of the few occasions where I would actually encourage you to look outside yourself for some feedback, either from other people or from different types of assessments. The reason I encourage this strategy is that it's often easier for other people to see your talents than it is to see your own. So if people compliment you on something you've done, be careful not to invalidate or discount what they've said; instead, see it as a possible strength that deserves further exploration. Also, there are many types of assessments, ranging from academic and personality assessments like the Myers-Briggs or those tapping into multiple intelligences (athleticism, music/artistic talent) or skills like leadership ability. While such assessments can be a great starting point for learning about your relative strengths and weaknesses, I caution you against blindly accepting any external criteria as definitive, be it an assessment tool or someone else's opinion about you. Instead, observe the feedback you might be getting but check in with yourself internally to see whether or not what you're hearing about yourself "fits."

Avoid labels

Also, another word of caution: when learning about who you really are, be careful not to describe yourself using broad brush strokes—labels like "I'm smart (or not)," "I'm creative (or not)," "I'm trustworthy (or not), " or "I'm athletic (or not)," etc. One of the problems with labels like these is that they don't allow you to get to know yourself deeply enough because they define you in a much too shallow way. For example, while I have a doctorate in clinical psychology, if you put me in an organic chemistry or accounting class, my head would hurt. So am I "smart" or not? Instead of blanket labels, isn't it much more informative for me to discover that my mind definitely prefers the "big picture" analytic thinking related to psychology rather than the linear mathematical thinking that chemistry and accounting require? Similarly, consider labeling someone as creative or not. There are so many different ways someone can be creative. Where some people may be creative through artistic endeavors or handcrafts, others may be creative in the ways they solve mathematical or chemical equations. If you avoid using blanket labels and focus instead on describing your capabilities more specifically in terms of which situations and in which ways you may be smart, creative, athletic, musical, quiet or outgoing, adventurous or reserved, you will get a much richer understanding of who you are and what you are meant to do.

Think back to when you were a kid

Another rich source of information about who we really are often comes from thinking back to your childhood—especially before the ego/database assumed more of a dominant role in your life, typically around late elementary school. If you think back to your earliest years, ask yourself (or those who knew you best) about the activities you enjoyed doing most and how people would have described your personality. Were you someone who was drawn to imaginative play, making music, building, being active, or more solitary activities like making puzzles or drawing? Would people have described you as energetic and outgoing or more soft-spoken and someone who could easily entertain yourself? Were you naturally neater, more precise, and a "rule follower", or did the household clearly know when you were around because you left a trail wherever you went or were comfortable challenging authority?

As you got further into school, did you enjoy it? Why or why not? Were there certain subjects that just came more easily to you or where you didn't have to work hard to come up with topics for projects or papers? What were those subjects, why were they easy for you? Which aspects of those courses did you enjoy most? Go through the same process for those subjects that were toughest for you.

When we are young, we are typically more connected to our unique consciousness because we haven't developed the self-consciousness that often accompanies the ego/database becoming more dominant in our lives. Precisely for this reason, reflecting back on your early years can be a great source of information about some of the natural inclinations in your acorn.

Start observing your reactions to things

Another important skill to develop in order to learn about your unique consciousness is to become more in tune to your reactions to things that occur in your daily life. For instance, you may have a reaction to a current news story, a conversation you overhear or an interaction you observe between people in public. In these situations, don't just stop at forming a general opinion of the situation; instead, put the effort in to ask yourself not only what your position on the topic is but why. Ask yourself if you were in charge what, if anything, would you do differently? If you were forced to come up with a solution, what would you do and why?

Similarly, be aware of your reactions to TV shows or movies that you watch or books you read. If you particularly liked or disliked one of these, don't just stop there. Dig a little deeper and ask yourself what it was that you liked or disliked. What characteristic, value, or viewpoint from your unique consciousness might your reaction reflect? Do the same thing with people in your life that you particularly admire versus those you struggle to respect. What is it about those people that you admire versus those you don't? What is it about the way they approach life or their views and philosophies that you wish to emulate or not? What characteristics about yourself do you think your reactions reflect?

Become more conscious of your core values

An important part of your unique consciousness is the set of core values that resonate most deeply with you. Your values reflect what's most important to you and your unique purpose here. These are very important guides to helping you live a meaningful life. The image I like to use when talking about our values and our real selves is that of a sailboat. Imagine a big old wooden sailboat. Our core values that originate from our unique consciousness are like the ballast of the ship. The ballast, located in the bottom center part of the ship, helps keeps the ship stable and helps keep its course. The same is true for your values. Living your life on a daily basis in a way that is more consistent with those values that resonate most deeply with you will lead to a richer sense of meaning and purpose in your life.

To discover which values are most central to who you really are, first think again about people in your life whom you admire. What values do they live their lives by? Do the same with people to whom you have a strong negative reaction. Secondly, look below at the grid of values. Pick the 10 values that resonate most strongly or strike a "chord" with you. Next put those values in order of importance from 1-10.

Grow Beyond Your Mind–Values Grid

Acceptance	Compliance	Effectiveness
Achievement	Conformity	Efficiency
Adventure	Connection	Empathy
Affection	Consciousness	Enjoyment
Altruism	Conviction	Endurance
Ambition	Cooperation	Entrepreneurship
Assertiveness	Courage	Equality
Attentiveness	Creativity	Ethics
Attractiveness	Dependability	Excellence
Awareness	Depth	Exploration
Belonging	Determination	Expressiveness
Comfort	Discipline	Fairness
Commitment	Diversity	Faith
Community	Drive	Family
Compassion	Duty	Fidelity
Freedom	Inquisitiveness	Loyalty
Friendship	Insightfulness	Mastery
Generosity	Inspiration	Meaning
Gratitude	Integrity	Mindfulness
Growth	Intelligence	Motivation
Harmony	Intimacy	Nature
Hard work	Introspection	Openness
Health	Intuition	Optimism
Honor	Justice	Order
Humility	Kindness	Patience
Impact	Knowledge	Passion
Independence	Leadership	Patriotism
Individuality	Learning	Peace
Industry	Logic	Perseverance
Ingenuity	Love	Pleasure
Power	Security	Spontaneity
Practicality	Self-actualization	Strength
Prosperity	Self-control	Teamwork
Productivity	Selflessness	Thoughtfulness
Precision	Self-reliance	Thrift
Privacy	Self-respect	Trust
RationalityReliability	Sensitivity	Truth
Resilience	Sensuality	Understanding
Resourcefulness	Service	Uniqueness
Respect	Simplicity	Unity
Responsibility	Sincerity	Usefulness
Sacredness	Solitude	Wisdom
Sacrifice	Spirituality	

FIGURE 8a: Grow beyond your mind—values grid

Grow Beyond Your Mind
My Core Values & Daily Actions

Look over the list of values again. Out of all the values you scored a 1, pick the top 10 values that are most important to you and that you would like to emulate in your daily life and write them in the chart below. Then on a daily basis, think of one action you did that day that reflected each of those values. You will be amazed at how grounded you can become by living your life on a daily basis in a way that is consistent with your deepest core values.

My Core Values   My Daily Actions

1. _____   _____
2. _____   _____
3. _____   _____
4. _____   _____
5. _____   _____
6. _____   _____
7. _____   _____
8. _____   _____
9. _____   _____
10. _____   _____

FIGURE 8b: Grow beyond your mind—core values and daily actions

These values are a big part of the ballast of your ship. Living your life in a way that is consistent with them will help you stay on course to a meaningful life. Think of these values as a yardstick against which you measure your daily life. For example, if one of your values is spending time with family, ask yourself each day if you did something that reflected that value, even if it's a small thing like spending 10 minutes playing a card game with one of your children. Or if spirituality is a core value, ask yourself what you did during the day that reflected that value. Many of us get caught up in setting goals for ourselves, both long and short term. While goals certainly serve an important purpose, we can't always meet our goals every day, yet we can always do something small each day that's consistent with our core values. You would be amazed at what consciously living your life on a daily basis in a way that reflects your core values does to grow the "ballast" of your ship. Ultimately, you end up feeling much more grounded and "on course" in life.

Take the time to reflect upon these thought questions

Another strategy to help give you some insight into your unique consciousness is to reflect on the following questions. When thinking about these questions, try not to focus on what you "should" do or how you "should" answer—that would reflect more of the programming of your database. Instead, try to answer from your "gut" or what the voice of the unique consciousness is trying to tell you.

- If you had a totally free day (a blank slate) where you could create your ideal day, what would you fill it with and why?
- What topics or activities can you talk or read about for hours without getting bored? These are your passions.
- If you've lived in or travelled to different regions or cultures, are there certain environments where you feel more at home? If so, why? What was it about these areas that resonated with you?
- If you were at the end of your life looking back, what would you need to have seen, done, created, legacy left to be able to say, "That was a life well-lived"?

- If people were speaking about you after you passed away, what would you want them to say about you?

Realize we're all pieces of the puzzle

As you're learning more about your unique consciousness, I also hope you are learning not only to listen to your unique consciousness but also to trust that voice of wisdom. Doing so will not only lead you toward true contentment but it will also help ensure that the world benefits from your gifts and talents which we so desperately need. Remember the use of the puzzle metaphor from our earlier discussion of the unique consciousness. When making a puzzle, you understand that no one piece of the puzzle is any more important than any other piece. It bothers you when you're making a puzzle and you come to the end, only to realize you're missing one of the pieces. Regardless of whether it's the most colorful, elaborately designed piece or a "basic" solid piece, the puzzle doesn't work unless all the pieces are present. Our world works the same way. We all come with a part to play in the world and our purpose here is to figure out our piece of the puzzle and play it to our fullest potential. Just as no piece of the puzzle is any more important than any other, so no human being is inherently more important than any other—although this is exactly what the ego/database would have you believe. Now, I'm not saying that people don't make contributions that are valued differently by the world. What I am saying is that you need to separate the worth of the person from how society values or does not value their contributions. No person is inherently more or less valuable than any other—their worth is unconditional, based on the fact that they are a unique human being and have a part to play in this world that only they can play.

The other thing about a puzzle is that not only does every piece need to be present in order to make it work but remember it also needs to be in the right spot in the puzzle. When you're making a puzzle and you come across a piece that you're not quite sure fits in a particular location and you try to jam it into place, a couple of things happen. First, you usually end up damaging the piece slightly, but the other thing that happens is when you actually come to the place in the puzzle where that piece really belonged, it's not there to do its part. You end up scrambling to find where the misplaced piece must be and then start making adjustments. The same is true for people. Can you imagine how many people are "misplaced" in the roles they are playing in this world because they have followed the voice of the ego/database and done what they "should do" or what their family/society dictated they needed to do in order to be "successful?" Not only are these people not genuinely content because they never cultivated their true purpose, but the world has also missed out on the gifts, talents, ideas, solutions and inventions they might have brought the world if they had only followed the voice of their unique consciousness.

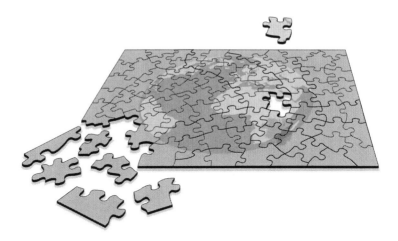

FIGURE 9: Everyone is part of the puzzle

The three simple steps to true contentment

The reason so many people never find contentment in this world is that they've gotten caught up in the ego/database and have not been able to find their way out of it. So, as we've discussed, the first prerequisite for true contentment is learning to free yourself from your ego/database and start listening and trusting the voice of the unique consciousness. After that, the process becomes much simpler:

Step 1: *Find out what's in your acorn*—use the strategies I've described to become a better observer of YOU to learn what unique talents, strengths, values and passions you were meant to bring to this world.

Step 2: *Figure out what you need to grow your acorn*—the next step is to figure out what you need to learn or experience in order to develop your unique gifts and talents.

Step 3: *Figure out how to share your gifts beyond yourself*—as human beings, in order for us to find true contentment, it's not enough for us to develop our gifts. In order to find life truly meaningful, we need to use the gifts and talents that we've developed in order to make a positive contribution beyond ourselves—be it to other people, animals, the environment or adding to a body of knowledge.

Ironically, that's how simple the path to true contentment really is—it's the ego/database that makes life so complicated. Unfortunately, for too many, the ego/database has become a trap and the master of their lives rather than the tool it was originally intended to be. The ego/database is an amazing survival and problem-solving tool. Its original purpose was not to be our master but to be a tool to help us manifest what was in our acorn and help us fulfill our purpose in this world. Let us now turn our attention to the database and learn how to get it to actually work for us instead of allowing it to be an obstacle on our path to contentment.

Phase Three

....

Manifesting the Real You by Using Your Mind Constructively

Understanding How Your Programming Creates Your Life

A universe of possibilities

The programming in your database (the beliefs and thoughts that you engage on a regular basis) plays a much bigger role in determining what your life ends up looking like than you may realize. One of the first ways our thoughts and beliefs create our reality is by functioning as filters through which our focus and attention are directed. Let me explain what I mean by this statement. The universe that surrounds us on a daily basis contains an infinite amount of data and possibilities. As we make our way through our environment, we may believe that we perceive a large percentage of the information around us. However, the reality is that our conscious mind perceives a mere sliver of the information out there and while our unconscious mind can pick up more information than our conscious mind can, it still can't begin to fully perceive and process the sea of data and possibilities out there in our universe (Siegel, 2012).

Our "shopping" list

Our thoughts and beliefs therefore serve as filters for our mind that allow us to hone in on certain information or possibilities.

Because of this filtering by our thoughts and beliefs, what happens is that, out of the infinite data and possibilities in our universe, our mind sees only that data and only those possibilities that are consistent with our thoughts and beliefs. It then brings into our life only information and outcomes that are consistent with our filters (our thoughts and beliefs). What is most crucial to understand is that there is a whole sea of possibilities and information that our mind is disregarding because of how our thoughts and beliefs direct our focus and attention.

To help clarify this very important point, take a moment to think about your thoughts and beliefs as if they were a shopping list for a grocery store. Picture yourself in a large grocery store. If you had to think about every single item simultaneously, your mind would quickly be overwhelmed. Instead, you may use a grocery list to keep you focused on getting the items you want. When you see an item on your list, you focus on that item (disregarding other items in the store, at least for that moment), you think about where in the store that item may be, you start making your way toward the item, you pick it up, confirm it matches what you wrote on your list, put it in your cart, pay for the item and ultimately take it home with you. Your thoughts and beliefs are essentially your shopping list for the "store" that is our universe, and your *unconscious* mind in particular is one of the best shoppers out there on a mission to bring home whatever is on your list.

The power of our unconscious mind

The amazing power of our unconscious mind to be such a good "shopper" for us has to do with the fact that it has at its disposal a wealth of knowledge and a talent for making associations, including the ability to recognize patterns and solve problems—the depths of which may be hard for us to even comprehend. Think about the unconscious mind as an army of the most amazingly talented, capable and dedicated soldiers you have ever come across, ready to serve you and use every resource at its disposal to bring forth whatever you're asking. With such an amazing resource at our disposal 24/7, it's hard to comprehend how our lives could be any less than ideal. The reason our lives often fall short of ideal, however, is that most of us have not remotely learned how to direct and manage this "army" of our unconscious mind effectively. We don't pay close enough attention to our thoughts and beliefs, which really are the "marching orders" for our unconscious mind, telling it what we want it to "shop" for and bring forth in our lives. Instead, most of us go through life rather unconsciously, letting our thoughts and beliefs flow from the programming of our childhood and past experiences.

Our unconscious mind will do what we tell it to do—literally

The reason our thoughts and beliefs are so crucial in creating our lives is that as powerful as the unconscious mind is when following through on orders, it is not good at rationally examining the merit of those orders before carrying them out. Instead, not only does it blindly listen to the orders our thoughts and beliefs are putting before it; it also does so *literally*, with little or no regard for the consequences of those orders. For example, going back to our metaphor of the shopping list for a moment, let's say you were going over to a friend's house for dinner and thought you would pick up some flowers for her, so you put "flowers" on your list and head to the grocery store. But when you get to the grocery store you see that not only have they raised the price of the flowers but that the bakery has just put freshly baked blueberry pies (your friend's favorite) on special. In this situation, you may very likely decide to go with the blueberry pie because it makes more sense and disregard the flowers, even though they were on the list. You would have made a conscious, rational choice to disregard the shopping list for a better alternative. If only the unconscious mind were as rational! Instead, as far as our unconscious mind is concerned, once something is on the list (a belief is put in place) then it must blindly follow its mission of getting that item, even if it doesn't make sense or help your cause in the long run. It's going to buy the expensive flowers you no longer really want. As far as our unconscious mind is concerned, its mission is to use everything at its disposal to create a reality that fits our beliefs at all cost! Like a good soldier, it's not going to question those beliefs but just accept them literally as orders for what it is supposed to create or obtain for you.

So the same is true when it comes to our thoughts. If thoughts like "That won't work" or "I can't do that" are on the shopping list, then in essence you have instructed your unconscious mind to go shopping for "lack of success" or "lack of ability," and it will do so in a very compliant, mission-focused manner, even though "lack of success" and "lack of ability" would not be items you would rationally want to purchase. Similarly, not only will the unconscious mind not question whether you actually want what you are directing it to get for you in the form of your thoughts, but it will also take your words quite literally. So for example, if you have thoughts like "I'm overweight" or "I'm lonely," it will go "shopping" for these states instead of realizing that what you actually wanted it to shop for was the *absence* or *opposite* of these states, namely "a healthy body" and "meaningful connections with people."

As far as the unconscious mind is concerned, its mission is to get you exactly what you asked for on the list—no questions asked. So if our thoughts and beliefs are the "shopping list" we present to our unconscious, take a moment to think about some of the thoughts that may go across your mind during a typical day. What items are you typically instructing your unconscious mind to go shopping for, and are they things you actually want? Now think about some of your core beliefs you may be aware of about yourself, others and the world. Some core beliefs may include "I'm not good enough" or "Life is supposed to be hard work" or "The only person you can really depend upon is yourself." By holding onto such beliefs, you are in essence directing the powerful army of your unconscious mind to do everything in its power to bring about a reality for you that fits those beliefs—even if it's destructive to your happiness. It's very important to understand that your unconscious mind will be tenacious in complying with your request because it thinks it's helping your cause. Remember, its job is not to rationally assess the orders it has been given (the thoughts that you engage or core beliefs that have been programmed in the database); instead, it is to follow them literally, word for word, and it has an amazing collection of strategies, tools and tactics (subtle and not so subtle) for doing so.

Some of the tactics our unconscious mind uses to fulfill your requests

So once certain core beliefs get programmed in your database and you develop certain habits and patterns in the way you think based on your experiences beginning in childhood, your unconscious mind is then off to the races, trying to create a reality for you that fits your thoughts and beliefs. Some of its favorite tactics are described below.

One phenomenon that reflects the tactics of our unconscious mind is one you may have heard of: the *self-fulfilling prophecy.* Once our database is programmed with certain core beliefs, our mind is happiest when our reality fits this programming, even if it's something we wouldn't consciously want. When our core beliefs and reality match-up, our unconscious mind feels as if it has successfully complied with our "orders" or requests and "all is right with the world." However, when there is a discrepancy between our reality and our core programming, our mind experiences a sense of angst we refer to as *cognitive dissonance.* Our mind does not like this feeling and it becomes extremely motivated to "rectify" the situation. Let's look at an example to see how this works. If I had the belief that "I'm not a good math student" programmed into my database, the first question I want to ask you to see if you really understand how our mind works is "Would my mind be happier if I got a 65 on a math test or a 95?"

The sad reality is that it would be happier with the 65 because that result or outcome would be consistent with my core belief (my programming). As far as my mind is concerned, when I get a 65, that makes sense and all is right with the world. However, if I should happen to get a 95, it's like an alarm goes off in my mind: something has hit its radar (something's not "right" with the world). Now the unfortunate thing is that in this situation, my unconscious mind's first inclination is not going to be to start questioning my core belief and adjusting it to reflect that I may in fact be a better math student than I had originally believed. Instead, it may first try to discount or invalidate the result by saying things like, "The teacher must have given everyone an A" or "That must have been a fluke or the easiest math test ever." Then, in order to keep the integrity of my belief intact for the future, it will influence me to do things to ensure bad grades on future exams, like not paying attention in class or stopping my homework once it gets even remotely challenging. That way, I will ultimately end up with a poor math grade and my mind will have been successful in bringing about a reality that fits its belief that *"I'm not a good math student"*—and it will think it's done a good job in helping my cause. Take a moment to think about the ramifications of what our mind does with the beliefs it is programmed with and what outcomes actually end up being manifested in our lives. Unfortunately, all too often it is literally the programming of our own database that is sabotaging our lives and creating the biggest obstacles for us!

Another strategy our mind uses to affect or alter our reality to fit our beliefs involves getting us to move toward certain situations or information confirming our beliefs while avoiding those that don't. For instance, if you have the belief, "I am smart," your mind might lead you only toward subjects or experiences that confirm that belief, while getting you to (subtly or not so subtly) avoid situations that may be remotely challenging for fear that the "I am smart" belief may no longer reflect reality.

Our mind can also influence our interpretations of situations to fit our beliefs. For example, let's say you have the belief that one of your coworkers is inconsiderate. If she walks by you quickly in the hall without even saying hello, your mind may jump on that encounter as more evidence confirming that she is inconsiderate. On the other hand, if your belief is that that same coworker is a considerate woman and the exact same thing happens (she walks by you briskly without acknowledging you), your mind is going to make a different interpretation of the situation. You may likely conclude that she was in a hurry or particularly stressed out at that time. Take a moment to think about how much influence your mind has on your reality by guiding you toward or away from certain experiences or people and by altering your interpretations of experiences throughout your daily life.

How the Law of Attraction comes into play in creating our realities

Many of you reading this will already be familiar with the *Law of Attraction* and how it influences what we end up manifesting—or not—in our lives. For those of you who are not familiar, I will give a brief overview of how this law influences our lives, but for our discussion I would like to frame the *Law of Attraction* as another force the "army" of our unconscious mind has at its disposal to help create a reality that fits its core beliefs and thought patterns.

To begin to really grasp how the *Law of Attraction* works, we first have to understand what the field of quantum physics has taught us about energy and the universe. In essence, what we have learned is that our universe and everything in it, including ourselves, is comprised of energy. Picture that we are walking through a sea of energy fields vibrating at different frequencies and that we are also comprised of energy ourselves. Now the fact that some things in our universe appear as solid, liquid, gas or empty space simply reflects different patterns of vibration. So while you might think there is empty space between you and someone else, there is actually a field of energy that just happens to be invisible to the naked eye (Lipton, 2005). If this concept is a little hard for you to accept, I would just encourage you to keep an open mind about it as I explain the relationship between our thoughts, emotions and energy.

When our mind engages certain thoughts, "positive" or "negative," we will subsequently experience certain emotions based on those thoughts. So for example, if you had a test in school coming up and you had the thought, "I'm never going to understand this stuff"—you would then likely experience the emotion of anxiety in response to that type of thinking. If, on the other hand, you had been studying well for the test and had the thought, "I've got this" in regard to the material on the test, you might feel challenged but would not experience the distress associated with anxiety. The key to understanding is that the *emotions followed your thinking* (Burns, 1999). Each emotion we experience is really just a wave of energy that goes through our system. Different emotions carry with them different electrical charges—positive, negative or neutral. So when you have an emotion, there is a certain energy frequency that is running through your body at that particular time. The frequency of the energy is experienced not only by you but by those surrounding you, as well. This phenomenon is why most of us have experienced a situation where we walked into a room where people were obviously upset or had just finished having a conflict and literally felt the tension in the room. When we say, "You could feel the tension in the air," our bodies are actually picking up on the different patterns of energy that the people who had the conflict are sending off into the room. In another example, have you ever been around someone who just seemed to have the perpetual habit of being negative? What does it feel like being around that person? Don't you usually feel drained afterwards, almost as if that person was sucking the energy out of you? Conversely, what does it feel like being around someone who is positive, comfortable in their own skin and just enjoys life? Doesn't it feel good? Don't you feel more uplifted and inspired? Again, it's the energy that they are giving off that's having such a positive effect on you.

In very simplistic terms, the way the universe works is that energies of similar frequencies tend to attract each other (hence the name *Law of Attraction*). Thus, negatively charged energies tend to attract other people, experiences, and things of the same negative quality, while the exact opposite is true for positively charged energies. For our purposes, it's most important to realize that it's the thoughts you engage that create different emotions and send different energy patterns through your system and into your surroundings (Allen, 1992).

Thinking ➔ Emotional reaction ➔ Energy patterns ➔ Attraction of elements in our universe

So if our mind gets us in a rut of negative thinking, it is literally changing the energy that is running through our system and subsequently changing the types of people, items and experiences that we attract or repel. By taking control of the thoughts we engage or not, we can subsequently take charge of the energy that goes through our system and what we end up attracting from the universe. The cycle of thinking ➔ emotional reaction ➔ energy pattern ➔ attraction is probably the most subtle, least understood, but also the most powerful way our mind ends up creating a reality that makes sense to it and that is consistent with its programming (no matter how dysfunctional that programming might be).

The key point to remember here is that your mind tries to create a reality that fits the programming of your database and that it's incredibly good at doing so!

Learning About
Your Specific Programming

Now that you understand the power of the database, the next step is to learn more specifically the programming of your own database. The key is to bring the unconscious implicit material into your explicit conscious awareness (Siegel, 2012). By doing so, you not only learn how to live life more consciously but you are also in the position to start "editing" the programming of your database so it is more in line with who you really are and your purpose in this world.

Learning about the programming of your unconscious implicit mind is a bit like being a detective. The first step is to look for clues. The most important set of clues actually comes from taking a survey of your life now. Ask yourself on a scale of 1 to 10 with ten being extremely satisfied/fulfilling and 1 being not at all satisfied/fulfilling, how satisfied are you in the following arenas of your life:

- Sense of self/self-esteem (feelings of worth, self-acceptance)
- Family relationships
- Romantic relationships
- Friendships
- Work relationships
- How you manage emotions

- How you approach conflict
- How you manage stress
- Your ability to problem solve effectively
- How you manage your personal space (cleanliness/orderliness)
- How you take care of your personal daily responsibilities
- Your overall health
- Your weight
- How you approach school/learning
- Your career/work life
- How you handle performance situations (work, athletic, school, etc.)
- How you respond to "failure"
- How you approach new situations/change
- How you manage money
- Your overall financial success

Taking the time to go through this assessment is important because your level of satisfaction or fulfillment in the different areas of your life will give you important information regarding the programming in the your database. Those areas of higher satisfaction would suggest relatively constructive programming in that "department" of the database, whereas areas of less satisfaction would highlight those that likely need more "editing." When I say department, it's important to remember how the implicit database is organized. While our conscious memory tends to be organized more chronologically (i.e., we have a sense that time has passed when recalling our childhood and the events of our life story), the implicit memory is organized more by neural associations than by time. Remember what I mean by neural associations from our earlier discussion of Pavlov's work with dogs, which demonstrated the principles of classical conditioning. Dogs naturally salivate when shown food. Prior to presenting the dogs with food, Pavlov would ring a bell. After a few trials, the dogs began salivating simply at the sound of the bell—the food and bell had been paired, or associated, in the dogs' minds. This relationship is what I mean by a neural association. When thinking about the database of our implicit mind, again picture a 3D spider web network of neural associations organized into departments by themes such as emotions, conflict, relationships, school, work, etc. Because the database is separated into departments, we often see the phenomenon where we may function very well in one area of our life (such as work/career) and not so successfully in another arena, such as relationships. It's absolutely possible to have gotten very healthy adaptive programming in one theme/area of your life and quite dysfunctional programming in another. Your level of satisfaction or dissatisfaction in the areas of your life will guide you toward those areas that will require the most examination and "editing" on your part to increase your overall level of contentment.

Once you have identified the areas of the database that need the most editing, the next step is to try to form hypotheses as to what types of information you may have picked up along the way. We do this by thinking about our childhoods, not only the environments in which we were raised (our family, schools, friendships and major life events) but also what was going on in the world during our formative years. Current events, the social/cultural media of the times, economic factors and other stressors can have a major impact on us and the programming we developed.

Let's start the exploration process with the broadest factors and move to your more immediate environment. When thinking about cultural events or stressors, realize that your parents or caretakers were also being impacted by these events, even if you yourself weren't directly affected. So if there were events like economic downturns or periods of unemployment for your family, the overall stress level of your home likely went up as well, which in turn would have impacted your database.

Questions to help you map out your programming

Take the time to answer the following questions as best you can. This will go a long way towards helping you map out the programming you received. In the next section we will talk about developing healthier, more constructive ways of thinking.

1) Let's begin with what was going on in the world during the first two decades of your life:

- What were the major current events during that time period?
- Who was president?
- What was going on in our country at that time?
- What was the economy like?
- Was our country involved in any major wars/conflicts?
- What were the major traumas of that time?
- What were the major health issues/scares of the time?
- How would you say your family or caretakers were affected by the above events?

2) *Next, let's move on to more of your immediate environment:*

- Do you know if you were the result of a planned pregnancy?
- How prepared would you say your family (both your parent[s] and other siblings) were for your birth?
- Where was your family living when you were born?
- Who lived with you?
- What was the living arrangement like (did you share a room, etc.)?
- How safe did the environment feel to you?
- What are four to five words you would use to describe your home(s) growing up?
- How would you describe the town/city you grew up in? What are the first four to five words that come to mind?
- Did you move frequently? If so, what do you remember most about each of the locations where you lived?
- How was your family doing economically during the first two decades of your life?
- Did both of your parents work?
- If so, did they enjoy their jobs?
- Were their jobs stable?
- Did they struggle to provide financially for the family?
- What were their job schedules like? Did they have to travel often?
- What traumas or losses did your family experience during your first two decades of life? What do you imagine the impacts of these were on you?

3) Now let's look at your parent(s) or caretakers. Who took care of you as a young child? For each person involved in your care, respond to the following questions:

- Think of the first four to five words that come to mind when describing them
- How psychologically "healthy" or grounded would you say they were, based on what you know?
- Do you know if they had any psychological issues or addiction/dependency issues?
- How safe did you feel in their care?
- How loved did you feel in their care?
- How responsive to your needs would you say they were?
- Did you feel heard and understood by them?
- Did they take an interest in your activities, opinions or thoughts about things?
- How did they discipline you? How often?
- What are the top four to five things you remember most about each of them?
- How was their health during the first two decades of your life?
- Did you lose any of them to death, divorce or abandonment?

4) Next, let's look at some more specific themes or departments in the database:

Sense of self/self-esteem (feelings of worth, self-acceptance)
- In your family, did you get the message that your worth was conditional upon something external to you, such as behavior, appearance, performance or following a certain path in life?

- Did you feel unconditionally loved and accepted for who you were?
- Did you feel loved by your family even if at times your behavior was considered "unacceptable?"

Friendships
- Who were your peers growing up?
- Were you in daycare with other children?
- What do you remember from your friendships during grade school, junior high, high school, college?
- Did you struggle to make friends or maintain friendships?
- How long is your longest friendship?
- Were your friendships relatively stable or drama filled?
- Did your parents have successful friendships?

Romantic relationships
- How would describe your parents' marriage? What four or five words come to mind to describe it?
- Would you say your parents genuinely loved each other?
- Did your parents stay married? If so, are you glad they did?
- What aspects of your parents' relationship did you admire? What aspects would you rather not replicate?
- Would you say your parents respected each other?
- Would you say your parents were able to trust each other?
- Would you say your parents could count on each other for support?
- Would you say your parents' relationship resembled an equal partnership or was there a clear power differential in the relationship?
- Did your parents work well together?

- Would you say your parents' relationship made you feel more encouraged or cynical about romantic relationships?
- What was your earliest romantic relationship? How would you describe it?

Work relationships
- How would you describe your parents' work relationships to the best of your knowledge?
- What was your earliest job?
- How did you get along with your co-workers?
- Do you generally work well with others?
- What types of people do you work well with?
- What types of people do you struggle to work well with?
- How often would you have conflicts with co-workers?
- How would they be resolved?
- How did you get along with your boss?
- How well would you say you take directions or corrections from someone in authority?
- If you made a mistake at work, what would you do?
- Were you ever let go from a job? If so, why?
- What was your longest place of employment?
- What was your shortest place of employment? Why did it end?
- Approximately how many different jobs have you had in your life?

How you manage emotions
- How well would you say your parents managed emotions?
- How comfortable with emotions would you say your parents were?

- What would your parents do when they were upset? How did they cope?
- Did you ever see your parents sad?
- How would your parents express anger?
- Would you describe your parents as anxious?
- What would make them anxious?
- Were either one of them worriers?
- How often were your parents happy?
- Were there certain emotions that were not allowed in your home?
- Did either of your parents use guilt to try to control or influence you?
- If you were upset about something how would your parents react?
- Would you feel comfortable talking to your parents if you were upset?
- How well would you say your parents understood your emotional reactions to things?
- Would you say your parents coached you in how to deal with emotions? In your opinion, were they capable of doing so?

How you approach conflict

- What did conflict look like in your home growing up?
- Was there frequent conflict or did your parents never fight in front of you?
- Was conflict more overt, with yelling, or was it more passive–aggressive, where you could just sense the tension in the room?
- Was there any violence in your home growing up?

- Were you frightened when your parents or family members would argue or fight?
- How well did your family resolve conflict?
- Would family members actually talk through conflicts or would they just expect family members to move on without talking things through?
- Would family members apologize to each other?
- What topics or situations caused the most conflict in your home growing up?

How you manage stress

- How well would you say your parents or family members handle stress?
- What would you hear them say or see them do to help cope with stress?
- How often were family members stressed while you were growing up?
- What situations or topics caused the most stress in your family?

Your ability to problem solve

- Think about the members of your family: how would you describe their ability to solve problems?
- What types of problems were certain family members better at solving?
- Would family members be easily overwhelmed by problems?
- Would family members worry about problems that hadn't even happened?
- Did anyone explicitly try to teach you how to problem solve?

How you manage your personal space (cleanliness/orderliness)

- Was your home clean and orderly growing up or more messy and chaotic (where on a spectrum would it have fallen)?
- Was any family member obsessive about cleanliness/orderliness?
- How neat did you keep your own room or personal space growing up? Were you forced to keep it that way or was it by personal choice?
- Would your family be comfortable having company over or would they get too stressed about the mess or chaos?
- How comfortable did you feel in your home environment growing up?
- How comfortable were you about having friends over? Did it seem like friends felt comfortable in your home?

How you take care of your personal daily responsibilities

- How well would you say family members took care of their personal responsibilities?
- Did any family members struggle with their responsibilities? If so, how? Who would pick up the slack?
- Could you depend upon your parents/family members to be there for you and take care of what you needed them to?
- What responsibilities did you have growing up?
- In retrospect, would you say your responsibilities were age-appropriate?
- How well did you manage your responsibilities at home? How about at school?

Your overall health
- Were there any family members who had significant health issues while you were growing up?
- How would you describe the overall health of you and your family members?
- Would you describe any of your family members as a hypochondriac?
- Did any family members use health issues to seek attention or other benefits?
- Overall, would you say your family members lived a healthy or unhealthy lifestyle?
- What would family members do if they were ill or injured?
- How would family members respond to you if you were hurt or ill?

Your weight
- Did any family member have significant weight issues while you were growing up (either over- or underweight)?
- Did you ever have a weight issue? Was your weight ever an issue at your yearly check-ups?
- Were there any family members who would diet frequently or talk about trying to lose weight?
- How would you describe family members' relationship with food?
- Would anyone engage in emotional eating?
- Would any family member use food as a numbing/avoidance strategy?
- Would you regularly have family dinners?
- Who took care of preparing meals?

- How much freedom/choice would you say you had over which foods you ate and how much you ate?
- How comfortable would you say your family members were with their body images?
- What kind of comments might you hear them saying about their bodies?
- To the best of your knowledge, did any family member have any eating disorder?
- How comfortable would you say you were with your body image growing up?
- Would any family members or friends ever make comments about your body or weight?
- Did you ever try to lose weight as a kid?
- Did you ever struggle with any binging or purging of any kind?

How you approach school/learning

- How important was school/getting an education to your family?
- How much formal education did your family members have?
- Did your family members enjoy school/learning?
- Would you describe any of your family members as life-long learners?
- How demanding were your parents about your school performance?
- How involved were your parents in your education?
- How successful were you at school?
- Did you enjoy school/learning?

Your career/work life
- Did both of your parents work?
- Would you say your parents enjoyed their careers?
- In your opinion, were your parents in careers that matched their interests and talents or did their jobs seem more like drudgery?
- How successful were your parents in their careers?
- How stable were your parents' careers?
- What types of things would your parents say about work (e.g., would they frequently complain)?
- How would you describe your parents' work ethic?
- Did your parents try to guide you toward a particular career or were they supportive of your own choices?
- How early were you encouraged to begin working? What types of jobs did you do while growing up?

How you handle performance situations (work, athletic, school, etc.)
- How did your family members approach (or avoid) performance situations themselves?
- How did family members cope with both "success" and "failure"?
- Would you be comfortable in performance situations? Were there certain ones that you were more or less comfortable in?
- Would you feel a lot of pressure to perform in certain situations?
- Did you ever feel like your self-worth was based on how you performed in a certain situation?

- How would your parents and family members respond to your successes? How about situations where you did not perform as well (relative failures)?
- Would any family members have the tendency to be overly critical of themselves or you?
- How critical would you be of yourself?
- If a performance situation did not go as well as you would have liked, how did you typically respond?

How you approach new situations/change

- What were some of the biggest changes you and your family experienced while you were growing up?
- How well did family members cope with change?
- What were some of the things they would do when approaching changes?
- Would family members help prepare you for changes? If so, what are some of the things they would do?
- How much change/variety do you like to have in your life? Do you shy away from change or embrace it?
- When you think of the word change, what are the first four to five words that come to mind?

How you manage money

- How well did your family manage money?
- Who took care of paying the bills, budgeting, etc.?
- Were there certain family members who were better at managing money than others?
- Were there frequent arguments about money?
- Would your family members worry about money?
- Would they frequently be in debt? If so, how did they manage it?

- Would they pay all their bills on time?
- What were you taught, if anything, about managing your own money?
- How well did you manage your money?
- How long did it take before you could successfully support yourself and manage your own finances?

Your overall financial success
- How financially successful would you say your family was?
- Did they have a negative attitude toward "rich" people?
- Did they have a "poverty" mindset themselves?
- What financial goals did your family have? Did they meet them?
- What types of statements would you hear about earning money or being able to afford things?
- To what extent was financial success tied to self-worth in your family?
- What role do you think financial consideration had in determining what jobs/careers your parents chose?
- When you think of being "financially successful," what image or picture comes to mind?
- Do you think it's okay to want to be financially successful?

Taking the time to reflect upon these questions is an important step in understanding the programming of your own database, particularly those areas that need the most "editing." Now that you have a better map of your mind's programming, let us turn our discussion to how to take the reins and learn how to program your mind effectively, so it actually helps your cause.

Programming Your Mind So It Actually Helps You

Now that you have an understanding of who you really are and how the database of your mind is a separate entity from your real self, the final step is learning to utilize the amazing tool you have at your disposal in a way that actually helps you manifest the life you were meant to live. As we have discussed earlier, the database of your mind has an amazing ability to create a reality that fits its programming. The problem is that most of us aren't even remotely conscious of the programming that's in our own database. In order to manifest our full potential, we absolutely need to become more conscious of the programming in our database and to start editing it in a way that is more consistent with our true purpose.

Even more important than knowing that we have the power to alter the programming in our database is first fully understanding that we have the freedom to *ignore* the ego/database if it's not helping our cause. Often our thoughts (which reflect the programming of our database) speak with such authority and conviction that we forget that we can choose not to listen to them if they're not constructive. True freedom begins when we know that we can consult and engage the database when it's helping our cause, but more importantly, that we can ignore it when it's not. Our ego/database is one of the most powerful tools at our disposal for creating our lives, and it's time we really learned how to use it.

Start with the core beliefs

When you're building a house, you first start with a set of blueprints, then eventually starting building the house from the foundation upward. One of the mistakes many people make is that when trying to change their thinking on various topics, they may try to "think positively" about a particular situation at hand, without changing their corresponding core fundamental belief(s). For instance, I have worked with several people who unfortunately, because of their experiences as a child, had developed the core belief that they were "supposed to be miserable" in life because that was what they had learned. So while they might try to consciously think positively in a particular situation, like going for an interview for a promising job, unless they address that fundamental belief ("I am supposed to be miserable"), their mind will unconsciously do whatever it can to sabotage their efforts and return their reality to being miserable. If you had a home that had cracks in the foundation, it would be fruitless to focus on fixing issues with the walls until the crack in the foundation was fully repaired. In the same way, in order to program your mind in a way that maximizes its effectiveness for you, you must start with your core beliefs. They are truly the building blocks for the life you are meant to create.

The most important core belief—the
foundation of the pyramid:
Do I have self-worth?

There is one core belief that dramatically changes whether your life heads in the constructive direction of your unique consciousness (who you really are) or the trap of the ego/database. That core belief has to do with where you derive your sense of self-worth. From the place of the unique consciousness, you realize that your self-worth is inherent in the fact that you are a unique human being, with a purpose in this world only you can fulfill. You are no more or less worthy than any other human being. Your worth is truly unconditional; thus, you don't need to do anything to "earn" your worth (you have already done enough simply by showing up on this planet). Also, because your worth is unconditional, it is totally independent of any of your accomplishments or anything external to you. Therefore, no matter what your achievements, your self-worth never goes up but it also never goes down: unconditional is unconditional. Imagine your self-worth safely placed within a vault. It is truly untouchable and nothing you need to be concerned about "earning" in your lifetime.

However, if you endorse the core belief that your self-worth is conditional, which unfortunately so many do, you are well on your way to being trapped by the ego/database. The ego/database would love to have you believe that your self-worth is conditional or dependent upon your achievements, appearance, performance, how you compare to others. Therefore, as your achievements go up, so does your self-worth, or "stock value;" conversely, if you don't perform as well, your self-worth can plummet. As long as you buy into what the ego/database is selling about your self-worth, you will have guaranteed yourself a certain level of anxiety or depression your whole life. Our self-worth is such an important need for us as human beings that when it's remotely threatened, we become extremely preoccupied with trying to secure it.

The reason the ego/database fuels chronic anxiety/depression is that it works on the "What have you done for me lately?" philosophy. So even when things are going well, the ego may give you a minute or two to pat yourself on the back for an accomplishment, but it won't let you rest very long, because there's always the next performance or comparison for which you need to prepare. In essence, when you buy into the ego/database's philosophy, your worth or value is always on the line no matter what. Therefore, you spend your life chasing or trying to ensure your self-worth—unfortunately, that becomes your life's "work."

The sad reality is that as long as you buy into what the ego/ database is selling, you never reach a secure sense of self-worth. You may get these temporary "hits" of self-esteem when you accomplish something or there's a comparison in your favor, but it never lasts very long and then you need another "hit" (another accomplishment or higher performance standard). The image that I like to use is an old wooden barrel that gets a big influx of water (you achieve something like earning over $100,000 for the first time). When that happens you temporarily feel "filled" (your self-worth is up). But with this type of barrel, there are actually small holes in the bottom of it through which the water seeps. As the water level decreases, so does your self-worth, and then you need another "hit" (you need to make $120,000) in order to feel "good enough." Many people fall into the trap of thinking there's going to be this magic accomplishment that's finally going to give them a secure, enduring sense of worth. But I can only assure you that as long as you believe in a conditional sense of worth, it will never happen. You will find yourself perpetually chasing your self-worth, only to never actually find it. It really is a wild-goose chase the ego/database will have you on—one that will never bring you genuine contentment or help you fulfill your true purpose in this world. Only by rejecting what the ego/database is trying to tell you and embracing the notion that your worth is inherent will you find true enduring contentment. Therefore, the first building block is:

> *Your self-worth is inherent in being a unique human being and therefore, your worth is equal to (no more or less) than any other human being.*

You have a unique purpose in this world that only you can fill

Once you truly understand that your worth is inherent, don't waste another minute of your life trying to "earn" it by listening to the empty promises of the ego/database. Instead, realize that you are a uniquely designed human being and your purpose in this world is to be YOU to your fullest potential. No other human being has the exact same constellation of talents, strengths, passions, interests, or ways of thinking as you. Remember we are all just parts of a puzzle. Your purpose is to discover and fulfill your part of the puzzle as completely as you possibly can. Rather than spending any time looking to the ego/database to learn who you are and what part you're here to play, turn your focus inward. Start observing yourself, your reactions to things, what you're drawn toward or not, the ideas that just naturally come to your mind and the things you are able to do effortlessly. Use them to guide you toward what you were naturally designed to do. Utilize the ego/database only in a problem solving/logistical role to help you achieve your purpose; don't let it tell you what your purpose is. For example, I knew a woman who made beautiful custom window treatments. The creativity she demonstrated in making the window treatments was part of who she really was—her true self. But without engaging her database, she never would have been able to figure out how much fabric to cut when designing and constructing the window treatments. She was using the database to help manifest something that came from inside her "acorn"—and that's exactly how the database was supposed to be used all along. It was always supposed to be a tool for us to manifest our real purpose and potential. It was never supposed to be our master, as it all too often ends up being. Therefore, the second building block of the pyramid is to realize:

> *You have a unique purpose in this world that only you can fill. Spend your time discovering and developing all the talents and gifts within you so you can share them with the world.*

Relationships

Human beings are meant to genuinely connect with and emotionally attach to each other—in fact, from birth our very survival depends upon how loved and nurtured we are by our caretakers. In the most ideal cases, our relationships with the closest people in our lives help us to both discover who we truly are and then develop our gifts to the greatest extent possible. Of course, that's the ideal and in reality that often doesn't happen for many reasons. First, for our caretakers to be able to provide such an environment for us, they themselves have to be fairly well connected to their real selves.

Think about our caretakers as "mirrors:" we initially start forming our sense of self through what we see reflected in them and their reactions to us. The more grounded and connected our caretakers are with their own true selves, the more smooth and clear their mirror—and thus the more accurately they can reflect who we really are. However, if our caretakers are still living their own lives trapped by their egos, their mirrors are going to have cracks and be cloudy. Therefore, the reflections of ourselves we see when interacting with them are going to be distorted because of their own unresolved issues. They may also encourage you to live life according to the ways of the ego/database because that's all they know—as far as they're concerned, that's how you're "supposed to" live life.

So when we're talking about relationships, the first relationship we need to resolve is that with ourselves. We need to realize that much of the information we may have in our database about who we are is likely inaccurate, a reflection of the relative dysfunction of our caretakers and our early environment, including our society and culture. We also need to realize to what extent we were taught to follow the ways of the ego/database, both in defining ourselves and programming what it means for us to be successful. The more conscious you become of how your sense of self may have been influenced by your early environment, the more you can differentiate what aspects reflect your true self and which are related more to the programming you acquired growing up. You can also consciously choose to reject the ego/database's definition of what it means to be successful and instead live life more connected to the unique consciousness and your true purpose.

Relationships look very different from the perspective of the unique consciousness versus the ego/database. The ego/database would have you believe that who you are is dependent upon some external criteria, how you compare to others, or how others define you. Unfortunately, because the ways of the ego/database are so conditional, relationships often take on a dysfunctional dynamic. They frequently end up being about playing different roles or "games" involving power, control, manipulation or "using" people for your own gain. Trust and a sense of safety (psychological, emotional and even physical at times) are often compromised. In such dynamics, you often don't feel like you have the freedom to just be who you really are, but rather that you must fit a certain mold or criteria that other people have set up for you. You also struggle to just accept other people for who they are and instead try to get them to act and function in ways that you deem most appropriate or preferable. Relationships often feel like work and leave you feeling drained, resentful, threatened, insecure, stifled or exhausted on many levels.

When you learn to live life from the place of the unique consciousness, relationships feel very different. You understand that we're all just pieces of this huge puzzle that makes up our world. You have a part to play; I have a part to play. No one piece is more important than any other and the puzzle only works when all the pieces are present. I also don't need to worry about you playing my part better than me—in essence, I've got dibs on being "me." I also understand it would be fruitless for me to try to spend any time trying to be a better YOU than you. When you're connected to your unique consciousness, you understand that your purpose in life is to be YOU to your fullest ability (to fulfill your piece of the puzzle as completely as possible). You also understand that it's actually in your best interest to empower others to be who they truly are because that's how the puzzle works the best for everyone.

It's very important for you to also realize it's not for you to dictate who other people are or "should" be but rather just to celebrate and nurture who they naturally are and help them discover and fulfill their part of the puzzle.

When you really start understanding how to handle relationships from the perspective of the unique consciousness, you will experience a whole different sense of freedom and growth from anything you may have ever experienced before. You feel truly free to be who you are and have a desire to develop your gifts and talents so you can share them with the world. You also just want other people to be themselves and learn to appreciate and accept them for who they are. You feel a genuine, enduring sense of security and realize you never have to feel threatened by other people. You enjoy people on a different level and are much less susceptible to getting swept up in games of control, dominance and manipulation. You will find that you can connect with people in deeper, more genuine ways. However, you will also find that there will be people you just naturally gravitate toward more or who just "get you" better than others (those with whom you just have more chemistry). Think about those people as "fitting" better with your parts of the puzzle. There will be others you just don't understand as well and that's okay— just think of them as being a piece in a different part of the puzzle from you. The key is to just accept them for who they are – don't fall into the trap of trying to make them fit your part of the puzzle.

Remember what we learned about relationships from our earlier discussion of observing groups of toddlers at play. Toddlers are old enough that you can really start to see their personalities and interests. Because they are not yet inhibited by any self-consciousness that tends to set in during elementary school, they are also free to be themselves to the fullest. If you watch a group of toddlers on a playground, you will see them engaged in a variety of activities like playing in the sand, running around or going up and down the slides. You will see their different temperaments and aspects of their personalities. But you will also see that toddlers tend to have their "buddies"—friends that they prefer to hang out with or just click with better than others. You may often see them even holding hands with those with whom they're closest.

That's really the recipe for handling relationships—just be who you are to the fullest, accept others for who they are, and gravitate toward those with whom you have the greatest sense of natural connection. Toddlers tend to understand this. It's only when we get older and our egos get involved that we tend to complicate relationships. The ego will have you thinking that to manage relationships you have to be and act a certain way, look a certain way, be interested in certain things, play certain roles, etc. in order to engage in relationships with people. Unfortunately, the ego's methods only lead to rather shallow, disappointing relationships that often feel more like work. It's only by being more grounded in your unique consciousness that genuine, deeply connected and enduring relationships are formed. Therefore the next building block of the pyramid is:

Relationships are about valuing and being YOU to your fullest potential while appreciating others and empowering them to do the same.

Emotions (they've gotten a bad rap)

Emotions are an incredible tool for helping us navigate life, but all too often they are not managed or utilized well at all. Unfortunately, emotions generally have gotten a bad reputation. There's often a negative connotation to describing someone as "emotional," while people who strive to keep their emotions at bay are frequently viewed as being stronger. But to really maximize our development, we need to start learning how to not only become more aware and accepting of our emotions but also how to listen to their guidance. One of the metaphors I like to use when thinking about emotions is viewing them as another sense like sight, hearing, taste, and touch. The reason evolution has equipped us with these senses is that they help us navigate life successfully and have dramatically increased our ability to survive. The same is true for our emotions. If we learn to listen to them, they could be an incredible source of information for helping us navigate life (Marra, 2005).

But as a species, we human beings frequently make emotions much more complicated than they ever need to be. In fact, animals tend to handle emotions much better than humans do because they just have them. However, humans, in our infinite wisdom, have decided that we don't like certain emotions like anxiety, fear and sadness so we're just not going to "have" them. First of all, that would be like us driving down the road and cutting off half of our visual field. Obviously, we wouldn't do that because we not only need to see the nice smooth road ahead of us but we also need to see the guy about to pull out in front of us—we need to see both the "good" and the "bad" in order to navigate the road successfully. The same is true for emotions. We need to be okay with experiencing the whole range of human emotions, from the "positive" ones to the "negative" ones. What many of us do, however, is decide that we don't want to experience certain negative emotions. But unfortunately, that's simply not how emotions work—we can't just decide not to have certain ones. They don't just go away because we don't want them. If we're not going to allow them just to happen, like animals do, then the next option we have is to try and come up with some avoidance strategy. These avoidance strategies are what really complicate our lives as far as emotions are concerned. We have created a plethora of these avoidance strategies like workaholism, perfectionism, alcoholism (any substance abuse), obsessive worry, being obsessed with body image, earning money, status—really any compulsion. We've also developed the strategy of having secondary emotions. Secondary emotions are emotions we choose to have instead of experiencing certain primary emotions. For example, rather than feel fear or sadness many people prefer to feel anger instead (the anger is *secondary* to the fear or sadness [the *primary* emotion]). Anger is one of our most common secondary emotions. Many people prefer experiencing anger because it comes with powerful energy and strength versus the sense of vulnerability that often accompanies fear or sadness. One of the problems with secondary emotions is that they often complicate our interactions with people and prohibit us from understanding what's really going on with our primary emotions. The many problems with other compulsive avoidance strategies are more obvious (Marra, 2005).

So avoiding emotions not only leads to its own set of complications for our lives, it also keeps us from really understanding our emotions, which can be a very wise source of guidance and knowledge about our true selves. In order to reach our full potential, it's crucial for us to change our relationship with our emotions—instead of trying to block certain ones, the key is for us to learn to just let them happen. We need to understand that emotions are just energy that wants to flow through our system. The mistake we make is that we try to block these emotions rather than just letting the energy run its natural course. Think back to the image we discussed earlier about a large rushing river with whitewater. Take a moment to imagine that you're smack right in the middle of this river. How does that feel? Most would describe feeling overwhelmed and a fear of being "swept away" by the current. You may try to block/dam up the river or make an even more futile attempt at stopping it with your hands. These "avoidance" strategies would not only be exhausting, they're also ineffective at best and destructive at worst. The key is to get to a place where you can get out of the way of the river and just let it flow as it may.

In order to do just that, again imagine the exact same river with the same whitewater and current, but now picture yourself on a nice sturdy high bank, well above the river where you would be beyond its reach. From that vantage point, you can now sit perfectly still, even as the river rages past you. You can breathe freely and just let the river run its course, merely observing what's in it as it does. If the waves and whitewater of the river represent your emotions, you can now just watch their ebb and flow as the energy of the emotions comes into and then out of your system. What's really important is to learn to not block the flow of the energy— just watch and listen to what the emotions are trying to tell you.

The most prominent primary emotions, including anxiety, fear, anger, sadness, frustration, happiness and love, all have a basic message that they're trying to share with us. Let's take a look at some of the more common ways these emotions are trying to guide us in our life.

Anxiety

One of the evolutionary purposes of healthy anxiety (as compared to obsessive worry, which is an avoidance strategy) is to help us prepare for something in the future. It's anxiety about winter coming that prompts a squirrel to collect nuts. If he wasn't at all anxious about the cold weather coming he might be up the creek when winter came. It's a certain level of anxiety about the end of the month coming that prompts us to send out the rent check. If you're in school, it's anxiety about an upcoming test that may prompt you to study. Healthy anxiety, therefore, motivates us to take action for a future event. It also helps us to kick it into gear to help perform at our best.

Fear

Many people confuse anxiety and fear. The main difference between anxiety and fear is that while anxiety helps prepare us for a future challenge, the message of fear is that there is an immediate danger or threat that requires our attention and/or action. Our reaction to fear is our *fight-or-flight* response that evolution has given us to help us survive. It's an incredibly powerful response that's been very effective at helping us do just that. Imagine back in caveman times. You're hanging out by your cave, minding your own business, when a grizzly bear comes by. Instantaneously, your flight or fight response kicks in (those of our ancestors who took the time to think longer probably didn't survive). Our fight-or-flight response is a full-body experience. As soon we perceive danger, our body signals the release of adrenaline, cortisol and other stress hormones that lead to increased heart rate, blood pressure, respiration, muscle tension and overall alertness. There are major blood flow changes from our midsection to our major muscle groups. Our digestion gets interrupted because all energy reserves are going to our muscles and other factors needed for action, like respiration. There are also changes in our sensory systems—our pupils will dilate to let in as much light as possible, our hearing and smell become as acute as they can be, and our "sixth sense" becomes heightened. Basically our fight or flight response is nature's way of saying, "Okay, you are now as strong, fast and perceptive as you ever can be; good luck against the bear."

Our fight-or-flight response has been an incredible tool, without which our species would likely not have survived. However, one of the problems we have today is that we activate this powerful response far too often than it was ever designed to be used. The fight-or-flight response was supposed to be activated every once in a while when there was an actual threat (an actual grizzly bear). But think about how many times a day you may be activating this response—when you're running late stuck in traffic, your kids spill milk onto the new rug, your computer doesn't work right or you're thinking about an upcoming presentation at work. The problem with activating the fight-or-flight response in these situations is that there's no actual threat to your survival in any of them but your body responds as if there were because your mind is perceiving or interpreting the situation as a threat. Because the fight-or-flight response is so powerful, over time it takes its toll on your body, especially when it's chronically activated. The good news, however, is that as you learn to manage your mind more constructively, your fight-or-flight response will be unnecessarily initiated less and less often.

Anger

When I'm referring to anger in this situation, I mean primary anger, not when we use anger as a common secondary emotion (secondary to anxiety, fear, loss or sadness). With basic primary anger, the message it's trying to tell us is that there's been some sort of a violation—either of our person, property or something or someone we care about. Try taking over an animal's territory or disrespecting someone and see what happens (obviously I wouldn't recommend doing either). Anger prompts us to take action.

The interesting thing about anxiety, fear and anger is that they all come with an energy dump because all their messages involve trying to prompt us to take some action. Nature designed us well in that, when we experience these emotions, our bodies also respond with the necessary energy to help us complete any actions that are required to meet the needs we are facing. On the other hand, compare that energy response to what happens when we experience sadness.

Sadness

Sadness does not come with an energy dump like anxiety, fear or anger. Instead, it comes with a withdrawal of energy. The reason energy decreases with sadness is because the message of sadness is that there's been a loss or injury so it's trying to prompt us to retreat and take the time we need to heal or recover. You will sometimes see this response with dogs whose long-time owners have passed away. They will often go off by themselves to grieve and experience sadness, then slowly re-engage with people over time.

You can see how the profound differences in energy we experience with the various emotions prompt us to act in very different ways, which is one of the many ways our emotions try to guide us.

Frustration

Frustration is one of those emotions that many of us would benefit from listening to better. The message of frustration is basically that what we are doing is not working. From an evolutionary perspective, it's trying to tell us that we are wasting our resources (like our time, energy or money). What frustration is trying to get us to do is to stop what we're doing and either evaluate the strategy we are using to deal with a situation or at least the timing of that strategy. Unfortunately, all too often many of us keep repeating what we were doing, only to deplete our resources with no gain but greatly increased frustration. When experiencing frustration, we would be much better served by stopping what we are doing, taking a deep breath, doing something different (if need be, seeking advice on what to do differently) or trying what we were doing at another time.

Happiness/Joy

If you really start understanding our emotions as a navigation tool, what the emotion of happiness is trying to tell us is to move toward the person, situation or experience that is fueling that feeling of happiness or joy. One of the reasons that the emotion of happiness or joy is such an important source of information is that it often gives us the greatest clues as to what's in our "acorn"—what clicks best with our talents, skills, passions and what we were really meant to do in this world. When you're engaged in an activity that resonates with something in your acorn, there's often a powerful sense of excitement, joy and positive energy. It's such a contrast to the sense of drudgery and the weight that comes with having to do something that you really were never designed or meant to do. So in trying to navigate your journey in life, gravitate toward those experiences that give you that sense of true happiness/joy (not fleeting fun) and whenever possible shy away from those that feel draining.

Love

Experiencing love—for ourselves, for others, for our work—is one of the greatest gifts we can be blessed to enjoy in life. It truly gives life a whole different level of meaning and purpose. When you experience the emotion of genuine love, what it is trying to tell you is that this person, experience or thing is something that is very important to you—keep it close to you, nurture it, protect and appreciate it.

Sidenote: differentiating normal anxiety from excessive worry

Many times people confuse anxiety and worry, so I wanted to take a moment to help you differentiate between the two. Anxiety is a normal, healthy emotion, while worry is one of the obsessive avoidance strategies we humans have developed. Animals experience anxiety, but it's only humans that obsessively worry about hypothetical events. We've talked about the purpose of normal, healthy anxiety but let me explain the purpose worry serves as an avoidance strategy. Let's say it was years ago, before we had cell phones, and I was sitting there in my family room waiting for my husband to come home on a snowy night.

If it was getting late and he wasn't home yet, I might start to worry about him. When I'm sitting there worrying, am I actually doing anything constructive to ensure that he gets home safely? The answer is no. But what my mind is doing is, as the "What if..." (worry's favorite phrase, by the way) images flash across my mind, my body starts responding *as if* those situations were actually happening. The body's response involves the initiation of the fight-or-flight response and large dumps of energy. The key point to understand about worry is that with the energy expenditure, I get the *illusion* that I must be doing something to ensure he gets home safely because I sure am "working" and burning energy. So the reason worry is so seductive to many is that it gives us the *illusion* that we have the ability to do and control things in situations where we really have little to no actual control. Obsessive worry ends up being a strategy to help us to try and avoid experiencing the feelings of *helplessness* and *powerlessness* that as human beings we generally really dislike (Bourne, 2010).

The key question to help you differentiate whether you are experiencing normal, healthy anxiety or obsessive worry is to ask yourself if what you are thinking is prompting you to take some action that may increase the likelihood of the outcome you want. If there is absolutely no action you could take, then you've likely gone over to the "dark side" of obsessive worry. Let me give you an example. If I had a student who was going to take the SAT in a week and she was anxious about the test, the anxiety she was experiencing might likely prompt her to take another practice test or two to help her prepare. In this situation, we would still be in the range of normal, healthy anxiety, because the anxiety prompted her to take an action that might increase the likelihood of the outcome she wanted (a higher SAT score). Now imagine the same student, only now it's an hour or two after she handed in the SAT score and she's sitting there thinking, "*What if* I answered that one wrong; *what if* they don't like my essay, *what if…*" At that point in time, is there anything she can actually do to increase her score on that particular SAT test? The answer is no—that's how we know she has slipped over into the dark side of obsessive worry.

———

I hope this discussion has helped give you a different perspective on emotions and increased your willingness to experience them more fully. I also hope you've gained more of an ability to differentiate normal, healthy emotions from the destructive avoidance strategies that only complicate our lives. So the next building block of the pyramid is:

Emotions are one of our best "senses"
for helping us navigate life and
learn about our true selves.

Stress

All too often when people hear the word stress, they tend to have a negative reaction and view stress as something to be avoided or at least reduced. Once again there's a very different experience of stress when you're living life trapped within the ego/database versus connected to the unique consciousness. When you're trapped in the ego/database, life feels almost perpetually stressful because you have the constant job of chasing and trying to maintain your sense of self-worth. Stress comes from the constant threat of losing your "stock value" (self-worth). You end up coming at life more from a mindset of threat than anything else.

From the vantage point of the unique consciousness, stress is experienced very differently. Stress is associated not with threat, but with *challenge and growth,* and it's what makes life interesting. As the famous stress researcher Hans Selye (1978) put it, stress is the "spice of life." Without stress challenging us to grow, our lives would become stagnant and boring. As you go through life, I would encourage you to adopt a "growth" mindset (Dweck, 2006), where you continually look to further develop whatever gifts or talents are in your "acorn." Don't ever stop trying to improve your skills, develop your talents or continue learning—it's what makes life truly fun and engaging. When you're connected to your unique consciousness, you realize you don't ever have to worry about "failing" or making a mistake because your self-worth is untouchable. Too often it's the fear of failing that keeps people from growing and challenging themselves and reaching their real potential. The key is to look at any moments of failure or mistakes simply as opportunities from which to learn—to learn about areas to improve on or how to do things differently in the future. Life is always about continuing to grow, learn and develop. It's only the ego that would have you believe you "know it all," have nothing more to learn, or that you're so superior at something that there's nothing else on which to improve. Don't fall into that trap—continuing to grow throughout your life is one of the things that helps make life so engaging and meaningful. So our next building block of the pyramid involves a different way to view stress:

> *Stress is about opportunities that challenge us to grow. That's what life's really all about— there are always new "branches" to develop, so never stop growing.*

Conflict

One of the reasons so many people have issues with conflict is that unfortunately, they have little experience with conflict being conducted well—that is, in a healthy, constructive way. Instead, many people's experience with conflict involves feelings of frustration, intimidation, fear/violence, passive-aggressiveness or threat of loss of a relationship. With experiences such as these, it's no wonder many people go out of their way to avoid conflict or automatically go into "fight" mode when they sense a potential conflict coming. The thing about conflict handled this way is that this is exactly how the ego/database would have you do it. In fact, it's the ego's tendency to fuel insecurity with feelings of threat and scarcity, and its fascination with power and control, that leads to conflict being handled not only poorly but many times destructively.

When you're more connected to the unique consciousness, you are by definition more secure and therefore in a much better position to handle conflict well. So what does conflict done "well" even look like? First, when you're more grounded and secure, you can recognize when someone is trying to have a conflict from the place of being trapped within their ego. That's when they would try to use tactics to "hook" you, intimidate/bully you, or disrespect/disempower you in some way. The more you can see what they're doing and stay grounded in who you really are, the less susceptible you will be to their tactics and getting caught up in a dysfunctional, nonproductive interaction. You will also be in a position to try and engage them in a more emotionally mature way, so the conflict actually reaches a productive resolution.

Some of the basics for managing conflict include avoiding personal attacks of any kind—they almost always lead to automatic defensiveness. Instead, focus on a person's concrete behavior and describing the impact their behavior had on you. Ask them to do something differently in the future if their behavior was that upsetting to you (Rosenberg, 2005). In order to really handle conflict well, it's not enough to simply get the other party to understand us and our needs; it is equally, if not more important for us to try our best to understand where the other person is coming from. Many of us are so focused on trying to be understood that we don't put enough time or effort into understanding the person with whom we're having a conflict. If you adopt the habit of trying to understand before being understood, you will already be well ahead of the game when trying to manage conflict well. One of the things I hope you've realized from our earlier discussions is that not only does everyone come with their own backgrounds, opinions and viewpoints, but that two people can even witness the same situation or event and have very different interpretations, based on their own databases. In order to effectively negotiate with someone, the more you understand where they're really coming from, the more successful you will be. You then need to be able to communicate your perspective and viewpoints in a way that does not attack, disrespect or devalue the person with whom you're interacting.

In addition to giving you some basics on conflict, I also want to share with you some of the benefits of handling conflict well. Whether you are parenting children, managing a home, or running a company or a community, there's a range of tasks and needs to be accomplished. Every human being is going to bring a unique perspective on any given situation, based upon factors such as their background (the programming of their database), their gender, age, how their mind works, what they value, and how they approach the world. Some of our greatest leaders, such as Abraham Lincoln, understood the value of surrounding yourself with people with different backgrounds and viewpoints than your own. While such diversity may create more conflict and be "messier" at first, in the long run, it's such diversity that allows you to complete more pieces of the puzzle than you could ever do alone or with people who only thought and approached the world as you do. While working with other people who challenge us in a respectful and constructive way can at times be frustrating, we are often able to create something better than we could have ever created alone, and that is conflict's greatest benefit. When either as parents, co-workers or members of a community, we are able to create something that has been discussed and challenged by all parties, so that what is created reflects the best parts and strengths of all our individual ideas and perspectives, that is the ultimate achievement of managing conflict well. The more we approach conflict from the place of the unique consciousness versus the ego, the closer we come to this ideal. So let us remember the next building block about conflict:

Conflict, managed well, can help us create
things we could never have created alone.

Money

Money has unfortunately also gotten a bad rap for many people. Many people associate money with greed, exploitation, power and materialism, and vilify the "rich." The thing about money is that there is nothing inherently evil or bad about it. The trouble with money comes when it is used to serve the ego. But the problem isn't with money, per se; it's with the insecurity of the ego and its insatiable need to be fed at all costs. Again, go back to the spectrum on which people fall, from being connected to the unique consciousness (who you really are) at one end versus being trapped by the ego/database on the other. The handling of money looks very different at either end of this spectrum. At the far right end, when trapped by the ego/database, your end goal becomes accumulating more and more money, no matter what the cost. You feel like your self-worth is dependent upon how much money you have or if you have more than others. It gives you a sense of importance, power and prestige that the ego just eats right up. This is when the insecurity of the ego feeds greed, exploitation and corruption. The other downside is that no matter how much money you accumulate, the ego is never truly satisfied or content. You may have fleeting moments of happiness when you reach another financial milestone, but they quickly dissipate and you need another "hit" (e.g., to reach another milestone) to get the same rush. This phenomenon is why you see people acquiring millions and millions of dollars but it's never "enough." Whenever your primary goal is to accumulate money, you will ultimately be disappointed. Don't buy into what our culture and maybe what those around you are saying about chasing money—it's never going to lead you to true contentment and happiness.

Now, the thing to understand is that accumulating wealth and abundance throughout your life is not a bad thing at all, but it needs to come from the place of the unique consciousness. Let me explain. When you're grounded in the unique consciousness, your goal in life is to develop your gifts and talents to the fullest extent possible and then share them with the world. It's absolutely okay to become financially abundant in the process of developing and sharing your gifts. Some of the most financially successful people in the world are people who have done just that, like the late Milton Hershey, Bill Gates, Oprah Winfrey and even some young entertainers, like Taylor Swift, who have managed to stay grounded in who they are despite their success. In these situations, their financial success is a by-product of developing their passions to impact the world in their own ways. The primary goal was to develop their gifts to make what they perceive as a positive, meaningful impact on the world. They also happened to become financially successful in the process. The other key difference is that when you're grounded in the unique consciousness, you don't let your level of financial success define your self-worth. You realize that who you are and your self-worth are independent of your financial portfolio. Whether your assets go up or down, your self-worth remains solid. There is nothing that needs to be "fed," as is the case when someone is trapped by the ego/database.

The other important thing that people grounded in the unique consciousness realize is that money is meant to be a tool to serve and empower others. It is not supposed to be your master or your end goal. Money in the hands of people grounded in their unique consciousness has been a source of incredible good in the world, from building schools, libraries and hospitals to making medical advancements and helping address problems of hunger and poverty. Money has enabled people to help and empower others in ways that would never have been possible without it. That brings us to our next building block:

> ***Money is supposed to be a tool to serve and empower others—never let it define your self-worth or be your end goal. Focus on developing all your gifts and talents, then sharing your abundance with the world.***

Success

The ego/database would have you believe that success is about chasing whatever criteria it deems necessary (money, status, body image, etc.) in order to be deemed "good enough." Of course, you never really reach this ephemeral "good enough" status for very long, and then you are back on the perpetual rat race of trying to chase and maintain your self-worth. Let me try to save you years and years on this exhausting treadmill which ultimately leads to nowhere but disappointment, regret and a sense of emptiness.

True success involves finding an enduring sense of contentment and engagement in a life that can never be found following the ways of the ego/database. But it won't happen as long as you're buying into a conditional sense of your own self-worth. The hardest part of finding true success and contentment is first not getting trapped by the ego/database. Unfortunately, the ego/database can be like quicksand—don't think you can dabble in it without getting sucked in. You really need to make the fundamental decision about what you believe concerning the origins of self-worth. Are you going to buy into what the ego/database is selling you about your worth being conditional, only to spend your whole life chasing something you never actually reach? Or are you going to realize that your self-worth is inherent in the fact that you are a unique human being with a unique contribution to make to this world and then spend your life doing just that to the best of your ability?

If you choose to reject what the ego is trying to sell, the path to true success and contentment is, surprisingly, not that hard. Instead of spending all your time and energy chasing and trying to maintain your self-worth, focus instead on learning about yourself and discovering what's in your "acorn" (what your talents, skills, strengths, passions—things that come naturally to you—are). Once you discover more and more about what you were designed to do in this world, next find the "soil" you need to develop those gifts and talents (education, training, mentors, tools, certain environments, etc.). The final step to true success and genuine contentment is then to share your gifts and talents in some meaningful way beyond yourself—either with other people, animals, the environment or a body of knowledge. Therefore, our next building block is:

Success is found by first rejecting the ways of the ego/database and then following this simple three step process: discover what you were naturally designed to do, find what you need to develop your gifts and talents and then share those gifts with the world in a meaningful way.

Empowerment

True empowerment only comes from learning how to live life so grounded in the place of the unique consciousness (of who you really are) that you're no longer vulnerable to letting the words of the database define you and your potential. It's truly a place where you have learned to live "beyond your mind"—a place above your ego. From this place you now have the freedom to develop YOU to your fullest potential and make the impact on the world that you were always designed to make. You then get to become a true constructive thinker and use the database as the tool it was always designed to be, instead of being its servant.

When you reach this place, you will also realize that life's not only about empowering yourself, but using your gifts and talents to empower others. Once you realize that no one else can fulfill your purpose in this world, you no longer have to be threatened by anyone else being a better YOU than you. And please don't waste any of your time trying to be like someone else—it's really as fruitless as the oak seedling trying to be like a maple or a pine tree. Remember, we're all just pieces of the puzzle that is our world. The key is to fulfill your piece of the puzzle to the greatest extent possible. So when you reach the level of true empowerment, it's not only about empowering yourself: you realize that part of living life to the fullest is learning how to empower others to be who they are to the greatest extent possible, as well. Just like no piece of a puzzle needs to be threatened by another piece (every piece has its own independent part to play), you realize that not only do you not have to be threatened by empowering others but that the puzzle actually works best when you do exactly that.

Think about how different the world would be if more and more people let go of the fear and insecurity the ego breeds and learned how to live life constructively from the place of the unique consciousness. Not only would we eliminate so much of the negativity and violence in the world, but the world would also benefit from people living the lives they were designed to live. When people live their lives in ways for which they were naturally designed, that's when we see positive energy and creativity. Some of the world's greatest creations, inventions, innovations and inspirational works have come from people who were living the lives they were truly meant to live. It is my sincere hope that you learn to do just that, and if the information presented here has helped you do that in any way, I am truly grateful for being able to be part of that process with you. I leave you now with the final building block:

True empowerment is learning to live life "beyond your mind" and encouraging others to do the same.

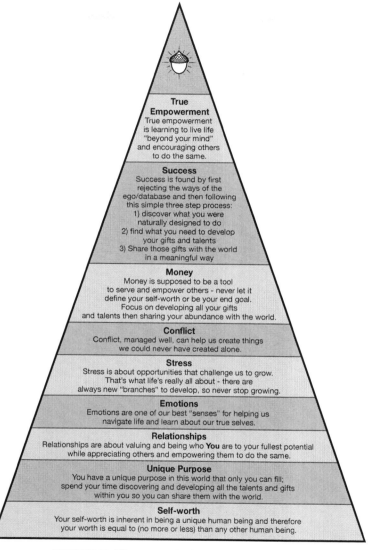

FIGURE 10: The pyramid of constructive thinking

http://growbeyondyourmind.com/pyramid

143

References

Allen, J. (1992). *As a man thinketh.* New York, NY: Fall River Press.

Benson, H. & Klipper, M. (2000). *The relaxation response.* New York: NY: Harper Collins.

Bourne, E. (2010). *The anxiety & phobia workbook.* Oakland, CA: New Harbinger Publications.

Burns, D. (1999). *The feeling good handbook.* New York: NY: Plume (Penguin Putnam, Inc.).

Dweck, C. (2006). *Mindset: the new psychology of success.* New York, NY: Ballantine Books.

Harris, R. & Hayes, S. (2008). *The happiness trap: how to stop struggling and start living: a guide to ACT.* Boston, MA: Trumpeter.

Hayes, S. (2005). *Get out of your mind and into your life: the new acceptance and commitment therapy.* Oakland, CA: New Harbinger Publications.

Kabat-Zinn, J. (1994). *Wherever you go, there you are.* New York, NY: Hyperion.

Lipton, B. (2005). *The biology of belief.* Carlsbad, CA: Hay House, Inc.

Marra, T. (2005). *Dialectical behavior therapy in private practice.* Oakland, CA: New Harbinger Publications.

Rosenberg, M. (2003). *Nonviolent communication: a language of life (2nd ed.).* Encinitas, CA: Puddle Dancer Press.

Selye, H. (1978). *The stress of life.* New York, NY: McGraw Hill.

Siegel, D. (2012). *The developing mind (2nd edition).* New York, NY: The Guilford Press.

Siegel, D. (2007). *The mindful brain: reflection and attunement in the cultivation of well-being.* New York, NY: W.W. Norton & Company.

Siegel, D. (2010). *Mindsight: the new science of personal transformation.* New York, NY: Random House.

Siegel, D. & Hartzell, M. (2003). *Parenting from the inside out.* New York, NY: Penguin Group.

Tolle, E. (1999). *The power of now: a guide to spiritual enlightenment.* Novato, CA: New World Library.

About the Author

Lisa Manzi Lentino, Ph.D. is a clinical psychologist in private practice who works with motivated individuals who want to discover their life's purpose, reach their full potential and create genuine freedom on a daily basis.

She graduated summa cum laude with a B.A. in Psychology in 1995 from Boston College. She then received her doctorate in Clinical Psychology from The Ohio State University. To complete her post-doctoral training, she worked at the ENRM VA Medical Center in Bedford, MA. Excited to be back in New England, she returned to Boston College to teach as an adjunct instructor for several years.

Lisa continues to live in Massachusetts with her husband and two children. She is also the author of the soon to be released children's book *The Littlest Acorn*, which encourages children to be true to who they are and appreciate their unique gifts. To learn more about her life strategies, visit Lisa's website, www.growbeyondyourmind.com.

Index

The page numbers for figures and illustrations are marked in *italics*.

V

values, *75, 76*
    See also core values

W

weaknesses, discovering, 70–71
work/career, 110–111

Y

YOU. *See* unique consciousness
your true purpose, 6, 29, 67, 78, 141–142, *143*
    discovering, 69–70, 117–118

If you're interested in learning more about
your specific programming and how to live the life
you were actually meant to live...
Visit our website
www.growbeyondyourmind.com
And take the

The Constructive Thinking Full Profile

What is The Constructive Thinking Full Profile?
- The Constructive Thinking Full Profile is a comprehensive and detailed self-assessment of your thinking and your mind's programming.
- The Constructive Thinking Full Profile assesses several different factors including: Sense of Self, Relationships, Emotions, Conflict, Stress, Money, Environmental Influence and Fulfilling Your Purpose.

What do you get after taking The Constructive Thinking Full Profile?
- Upon completion of the Constructive Thinking Full Profile, you will receive a 10-page report outlining 48 different scores that address these factors more specifically.
- The Constructive Thinking Profile enables you to identify certain categories where your thinking may be most problematic and directs you to more specific Constructive Thinking Supplements and other resources designed to help you think more constructively in those areas.

What are the Constructive Thinking Supplements?
- The Constructive Thinking Supplements are concentrated sources of information (ranging from 16-28 pages) designed to help you learn how to think more constructively in several key aspects of life:

Sense of Self	Money
Stress	Environmental Influence
Fulfilling Your Purpose	Relationships
Emotions & Conflict	

Start your journey of growing beyond your mind and
living the life you were always meant to live, and take the
Constructive Thinking Full Profile.

http://growbeyondyourmind.com/product/constructive-thinking-full-profile/

Proof

Made in the USA
Charleston, SC
23 January 2015